TORNADO! A FUNNEL OF FURY

A documentary of a disaster that came upon a town and it's people in one half hour of terror, including:

- Actual photographs taken immediately after the storm;
- Reliable statistics of other such disasters;
- Eye witness accounts.

*Tornado comes from the Latin word, "tornare", which means to turn.

TORNADO
A Funnel Of Fury

By Irene F Bakker

authorHOUSE®

AuthorHouse™
1663 Liberty Drive
Bloomington, IN 47403
www.authorhouse.com
Phone: 1-800-839-8640

Published by AuthorHouse 12/12/2011

ISBN: 978-1-4685-0738-6 (sc)
ISBN: 978-1-4685-0737-9 (e)

Library of Congress Control Number: 2011962057

Dedication

This book is dedicated to the many people who suffered loss of health, homes, and loved ones in the Tornado at Tracy, Minnesota, on the evening of June 13, 1968.

To Dr. Lee and others of the medical profession who worked endlessly to save lives and to ease suffering.

To those who came from near and far to aid in time of disaster.

With united hands and hearts it can well be said, "He hath loved his neighbor as himself."

JUNE 1968

S	M	T	W	T	F	S
						1
2	3	4	5	6	7	8
9	10	11	12	13	14	15
16	17	18	19	20	21	22
23 30	24	25	26	27	28	29

Preface

A very violent and destructive windstorm hits suddenly and often with little, if any, warning. The funnel shaped cloud in this case was white, for it had swallowed up huge quantities of water from Lake Sarah.

Thunder and lightning, rain and hail often accompany the rotary windstorm. Then roars the great sky like a million freight cars above. And then it hits, and whirls, and takes with it in a matter of moments, homes and cars, trucks and trains, and trees that have clung by their roots for hundreds of years previous.

Worst of all, by far, the tragedy of human life lost, nine of them this time, and countless others wounded.

It took years to work and build and gather together the material possessions that are now forever gone, claimed by the unwelcome funnel.

Thus it was on that dark summer evening at Tracy, my hometown. Should you sense any sentiment ahead, then consider if you will, what you would feel if this were your hometown. For here I was born in a building damaged by this storm, and here I went to school in one completely destroyed by it. These people who suffered and some of them who died, I knew quite well.

It has been said that one must go through a war to really understand war. I believe a similar statement could be said about a tornado.

It is my desire to leave the pages of stories and photos in this book that it will not be forgotten what can happen anywhere, to anyone, at any time; with my sincere hope that all will be prepared for it, and my deepest prayer that it will not happen again to anyone.

The author

Driving down Highway 14
West from the Twin Cities about the
Distance of 150 miles, you come upon the quiet and still
Beautiful city of Tracy. Here it was, unheard of most
Likely to most people around the United States, until
That night of June 13, 1968. The next day, however,
The news flashed on radio and television stations
Through the states and even overseas, of the
sudden disaster that came and destroyed and
killed and left homeless. People came and saw
and helped, and helped more, until a town
that looked hopeless and helpless
turned into a town of many new homes
and buildings; where love and hard work
became mingled together to build again
a place where people took up life again
and lived neighbors again, trying to forget the horror of that dreadful night. You
will still find many here to jump when the fire
whistle blows; who watch the sky for any sign of a
storm. The imprint of this tornado on each individual is
different---but none here will ever forget that night.

Welcome to Tracy
World's Only Box Car Days

Since 1927, Tracy has celebrated on each Labor Day. A colorful mile long parade starts at 1:00 sharp and is led by one of the town's most prominent citizens, Dr. Warner Workman, M.D. who until the past couple of years, rode horseback.

Beautiful floats and bands from nearby towns, as well as horseback riders draw thousands of visitors each year. There are rides on the midway for the young, and the young at heart, as well. Food and carnival stands line the streets and old friends meet once more to reminisce. A big show with a well-known actor or musician may be the main attraction. The climax of it all is the crowning of Miss Tracy, Boxcar Day Queen, in all her beauty.

Less than three months after the great tornado came to town, Tracy showed itself still capable of its yearly celebration. In fact, it was a bigger and better day than ever before!

Yes, indeed, life must go on!

Some Area Headlines

9 killed, hundreds of homes gone in Tracy twister

Tornado Rips Up Tracy; 9 Dead

Tracy ponders: Why?

Grim scene remains

TORNADO: The Long Wait

Alert Credited with Saving Lives

Donations wanted for Tracy people

$10,000 Received to Aid City In Cleanup for Tornado Victims

A Little Of History

Tracy is located in the southern part of Lyon County. It is in Monroe Township. It has a population of 2500. It was founded by the Winona and St. Peter Railroad Company in the year 1875. They called it "Shetek Station" first, but later named it Tracy after a director of the Chicago and Northwestern Railway Company.

The "railroad town" had a population of 1210 in 1885. It consisted of a warehouse, hotel, store, hardware store and a millinery shoppe at that time. By 1890 it had grown to 1400.

Much of the best farmland in the United States lay around the Tracy area. Many of the farmers in this part of the state lost their entire crops in 1873 when the grass-hoppers invaded the area.

Today Tracy still grows, regardless of the setbacks of the past. It has a swimming pool, theatre, and a bowling alley. It has a beautiful and well equipped hospital and home for the aged. The new Centennial Homes gives comfortable easy cared for homes to the other elderly low income folks. In the south part of the city is a new grade school and high school. Tracy is located only about 23 miles from Marshall, home of the Southwestern Minnesota State College.

The National Guard is also homed here, and the Municipal Building is a well kept public building. Tracy has one of the best Fire Departments around. The Public Library is also an asset to the city.

And The Clocks Stopped

"Whatsoever the Lord pleased, that did He in Heaven, and the Earth, in the seas and all deep places. He causeth the vapours to ascend from the ends of the earth: He maketh lightnings for the rain: He bringeth the wind out of His treasuries." Psalms 135:6,7.

Tracy lost at least a fourth of its' town and nine of its' beloved people. The Office of Emergency Planning in Washington D.C. offered the homeless food, shelter, and medications, as well as help to clear up debris and to repair wherever possible. In 1957 many Tracy people had helped out at the Marshall flood disaster and now the help was returned when the tornado hit at Tracy.

Civil Defense and National Guard units moved to town to help clear up the rubble. Hours of donated time and borrowed heavy equipment made the job easier and quicker.

Ham Radio Operators helped out by relaying messages to friends and relatives in other cities and states who were concerned for their loved ones in Tracy when they heard of the disaster there. A great many people contacted the Red Cross agencies, seeking to get messages somewhere in a hurry. It is certain that much tension prevailed on both ends until the messages finally came in.

The storm, probably the worst in Southwestern Minnesota history during the last half century, at least, soon became news even in faraway Viet Nam. There Tracy men heard it and were informed as soon as possible about their own families in Tracy. Bombing in Viet Nam and the Tracy Tornado probably resulted in some similar looking destruction.

Many civic and private organizations sent contributions of all kinds, money and clothing, furniture and appliances, etc., most everything to start up housekeeping again "from scratch." The Red Cross, the Salvation

Army, the Seventh Day Adventists and other church organizations as well, poured out help and love, compassion and mercy.

The first person to alert the Tracy Radio Dispatcher of the funnel sighting was Mrs. Melvin Koch of east of Garvin. The alert signal was immediately set off and probably saved the lives of many people. After turning in the alarm, Mrs. Koch followed the funnel to town. It hit about three miles from the Koch farm place.

"It was something I hope I never see again!" said Mrs. Koch. To her must go credit for the nine minutes between the signal alert and the time the storm actually hit town, when these lives were saved by the people finding underground shelter.

The giant white funnel swooped down on the city and played havoc for one half hour. It left imprinted on the minds and in the hearts of the towns' citizens a horror that can never be completely erased.

The clouds had built up over Lake Sarah and travelled to the southwest part of Tracy, after taking several farms along the way. City property damage was estimated to be around the $4,000,000 mark. Nine persons lost their lives and countless others were injured. Many more were left homeless.

History is said to repeat itself, and in this case it certainly is a fact, for there was an earlier tornado that hit the rural area on June 22, 1924. Four miles west of Tracy at that time a farmer was killed and others injured.

Many a story can be told about this 1968 disaster, but many more will never be known. What is known can best be told by those who witnessed the destruction. These stories, along with carefully selected photographs, may help to keep the facts compiled for those who survived this storm, and for future generations as well.

It is now history, history that left heartache, grief, fright and terror for many. It certainly is history that will never be forgotten to this area. It is a story of a small city with wonderful people who kept their town alive through many large obstacles. It is the story of a people who buried their dead, treated their wounded, rebuilt their homes, and kept on living.

Some Eyewitness Accounts

The following eyewitness accounts are taken from direct interviews with the victims of the Tracy tornado. Some are from people who were injured, others from those who lost their homes or other possessions, and still others from the more fortunate ones who were very close to the storm's path, yet not close enough to lose by it. Others viewed the funnel closely and fearfully.

As far as was possible the photographs of these people will accompany their story, so you may "see" these people as they tell you their experiences.

It was interesting compiling these events, but impossible for the reader to capture the expressions on the faces of these citizens as they relived the horror of the night that changed their lives.

Here follows, in their own words, the true episode of the night of June 13, 1968 at approximately 6:45 to 7:04 PM at Tracy, beginning at Lake Sarah where it was believed to have originated to the home of Mrs. Sadie Van Dusen in north Tracy, one of the last places to be directly in the funnel's path.

Charlie & Ada Lone

For 38 years "Charlie" Lone operated a resort on the east shore of Lake Sarah, the site of the tornado's beginning. Charlie's wife, Ada, said that there were some people on the dock who were watching the funnel as it formed. Someone told her that it started as a big white ball in the middle of the lake. The ball travelled to the north shore of the lake where it knocked down some trees. Then it went back into the lake, started over and then headed northwest of Tracy. These people didn't think that it would hit Tracy so they did not turn in an alarm.

Mrs. Lone saw the twister as it was over Tracy soon after it left the lake. It had taken with it a lot of lake water and some fish, some of which were found after the storm.

Charlie Lone

NOTE: Charlie passed away on November 16, 1970, at the age of 76 years. He had been blind for many years. Ada still lives at the resort.

This is the east shore of Lake Sarah and the dock on which people stood watching the funnel cloud form.

Mr. and Mrs. Steve Pool were retired farmers who had lived north of Garvin corner for many years. Only a few months previous to the tornado they had bought a big white house in Greenwood.

Speaking to Mrs. Pool about the night that their home was destroyed was a hard thing to do. She had obviously liked this home so well, and losing it and all of their possessions was hard. There were souvenirs and other things that could never be replaced, things that were acquired over their long married life. But their lives had been spared, miraculously. After looking at the crumbled wreckage that had once been their home it seemed almost impossible that they were here to tell their story.

Mrs. Pool's words were simply these: "I live it over every day!"

Steve Pool described the evening as he could recall it: "The whistle blew but we didn't know what it was for. We were only in the basement about two minutes when it hit! It took the house next to ours first. I was all black and my finger was badly cut. There was an old man running around outside who they had thought had been killed. He didn't even know what he was doing. The woman who lived near us was lying dead about forty rods from her house.

The funnel cloud dumped out the stuff it had picked up in Tracy out east of town. It was an awful mess! Since the tornado about 300 people moved away from Tracy."

Note: The crumbled bricks in the photo were all that remained of the Pool's home. After the storm Mr. and Mrs. Pool moved to live at

Chandler and are now at home in Walnut Grove. Mr. Pool's finger was badly cut on broken glass while the storm was ravaging, and it had to be treated by the doctor. Mrs. Pool was uninjured.

Pool Home   Mr. and Mrs. Steve Pool

Mrs. Dan Weaver feels very fortunate for not being hurt in the storm. She said:

"I had taken Bob (my grandson-in-law) to play ball after supper. It was sprinkling then. When we got there it was raining so hard that we decided to go home. We stopped at the West Side Grocery for cigarettes. While Bob was in the store it began to hail the size of eggs. A small boy came out of the store and ran. Bob said that we should go to the Nursing Home where his wife, Toni, was working.

When we got to the schoolhouse Bob didn't think that we were going fast enough, so he drove the car and almost hit the curb. We got to the Nursing Home and all went in the basement."

"I kept Kent, my great grandson, who was two years old, under me to protect him. The noise was a whistle. The storm didn't hit the Nursing Home. It took Bob's house and everything in it; also part of our house on Emory Street. None of us were hurt, which was a blessing."

Mrs. Weaver with Kent

Neighbors

For 25 years the Harry Cowell's had made their home in Greenwood. Mary Cowell spoke of the storm sadly, for she remembers her dear friends and neighbors who lost their lives in it.

"I heard on Channel 13 that a storm would hit southern Minnesota" she said, "but we kept on working. At night the wind went down and there wasn't any breeze. It rained and big hail stones came down. I saw it from my front porch and I thought, 'Here goes my windows!'

Mr. Cowell thought it was a train because we heard an awful roar. There was a train at about the same time. I thought it was a tornado. We went into the basement and then came back up and saw the funnel about a block and a half from our place.

I said to him, 'Come on! This is a tornado, and it's right here!' I got down there but he got to the basement door when a two by four hit him on the head. He had to have six stitches taken in his head.

Our basement was filled up and I was practically buried. I have always been afraid of storms. (My cousins were in the tornado of 1924. It took their home and all of the farm buildings. There were seventeen people in their basement that Sunday afternoon.)

Well, Millie Harnden was crying for help. She kept saying 'Get me out of here!' It must have turned her house all the way around. She died on the way to the hospital. Then Bill Haney came and asked me if I had seen his mother, Mrs. Dan Haney. We went over there and her house was gone. Her bright red couch was still there, and she was lying dead beside the couch.

Walter Swanson was by the third lot by the corner. He was lying back in the alley dead. He had always came and talked to us when he got through work. This time he had said, 'I am going down town to get something to eat.' I told him that there were tornado warnings out. He just laughed.

Mrs. Holbrook lived neighbors to us, too. She came up out of her basement and was killed. When Walter Swanson stood there, Nellie Van Meveren was going to get her mother and she told him to get in the basement but he just stood there. She got her mother, Mrs. Yoder and an eight year old boy, and made the boy get in a corner then her mother over him and she got over her mother. Both of the Grandma's were hurt. It took all of the house except the little part that they were in.

I remember that I put my head down in the corner because I thought I'd rather get my head hurt than to get my head caved in. I got bruised but I didn't go to the hospital.

Everything was gone, but we were alive! We had to wash all the clothes we did find because they smelled like fish. We found some fish from the lake in our yard.

At first we didn't think we would rebuild in Greenwood. We didn't know just what we'd do.

Everybody should have a storm cellar or basement and go on the side of the wall where the storm is coming from. I wouldn't live in a house without a basement.

Our son and daughter-in-law were out fishing when it hit and they felt so helpless when they saw it destroying places and they knew we were there and couldn't do anything about it. Their home was damaged but they have it all fixed up now."

Mr. Cowell added that someone had seen the storm funnel over the lake and they could see the bottom of the lake as the funnel sucked up the water. He said it took three blocks wide through Greenwood, but narrowed down to a block wide in town as it raised upward. He had not been afraid of storms like his wife, so was more reluctant about going in the basement, while his wife had hurried down there.

Mrs. Harry Cowell

The following is an account directly from Mr. F.V. Carey, the conductor of train No. 126, concerning himself and other members of the train crew whose lives were spared that night.

"Train No. 126 CNW Ry. arrived at Tracy at 6:55 p.m. or a few minutes before the tornado, and we were in the process of putting our train on yard track, when received information (via radio from yard crew) that a tornado was approaching.

Brakeman Milton King and myself decided to seek shelter in one of the homes adjacent to our tracks. I guess we ran back and forth three or four times between our caboose and these homes, thinking the path of the tornado was changing. (Optical illusion, I presume.)

Finally Brakeman King went to one of the homes and to the basement. I thought my best chance was in a drainage ditch near our tracks, and was just in time, as last time I looked it was just a couple of blocks away. It sounded like 1000 vacuum sweepers going all at once, but when it passed over me there was no sound. After passing it sounded like two trains coming together a 100 miles per hour.

Lots of boards hit me, one two by four hitting my neck, but somehow there must have been no force, as it would have cut my neck off. I believe that had I not been in the center of its' path it would have. When I got up there was one railroad car 20 feet from me and tipped over on its' side. Had the last car tipped over it would have landed on me.

We had 52 cars in our train and 26 of these cars tipped over. A few that were over a half block away from its' track.

It was raining and hailing so hard from Garvin to Tracy that we could not see ten feet from the caboose windows, otherwise I am sure we could have seen it, as it was not over two miles from our track. Our engines were out of the direct path of this tornado as was 26 head cars of our train.

Our train was made up at Huron, South Dakota. Members of the crew as follows:

- F.V. Carey, Tracy, Minn. Conductor
- Jim Bauman, Huron, S.D. Engineer
- Milton King, Huron, S.D. Brakeman
- Lloyd Melber, Huron, S.D. Brakeman

Ray and Alice Greenman live on 8th Street in Tracy. On the night of the storm, Ray was at work with the Railroad Company and Alice was home with three of her little grandchildren.

"We were looking out of the window," she recalls, "watching it rain and hail. It stopped raining and hailing and I walked away from the window. Then my grandson, Larry, hollered and said to me, 'What's that thing up in the sky?' so I went and looked and there it was, a great big tornado cloud!

Ray and Alice Greenman

I took the three kids and went in the basement, but then I happened to think that my neighbors, Minnie and John Sass, probably didn't even know that it was coming. So I took the kids and ran over there. When we got there Minnie was sitting in the living room and John was taking a shower. I told them that there was a tornado but they wouldn't believe me. They went and looked and then we all went into the basement.

There was a horrible screaming sound that lasted about too minutes, it seemed. After the noise stopped, Minnie and I and the kids went outside to see what it had done. Then we started picking up the debris.

I looked up and the tornado was coming back! So we headed for the basement again and stayed there about ten minutes more. The tornado had turned and headed northeast."

The Story of a Brave Boy

In their home in Broadacres, but a few blocks away from the disaster area, Barry Daniels, 13 year old son of Mr. and Mrs. Andy Daniels, played with his seven younger brothers and sisters, Vicki, Joel, Neil, David, Andrea, Mark and Kim. Their mother watched the storm approaching from the window. Their father worked away from home during the week for the Northern States Power Company, and was home on weekends. Barry said, "My mother hollered to me when she saw the storm approaching. She asked me what it was. I answered, 'It's a tornado! Get in the basement!' I had seen two tornado clouds before so I knew what they were.

We went in the basement and I told the kids to sit on the potato sacks. Mom started to count heads and two were missing. I ran upstairs and got them and almost threw them down in the basement.

Mom said that she was going up and I said, 'No, you're not!' Then Neil got frantic. We heard it roar for about ten minutes and then it was over. Then we went up and it was all white in the sky downtown. It looked like it had blown a lot of smoke away."

Barry Daniels

Hotel Windows Broken

Kermit and Maydrith Christianson, owners of the Hotel Tracy, took a good color picture of the funnel. Kermit told of the storm, "The tornado had missed our building by only about 50 feet and should still be seen about two blocks away. I took the picture in a short period of time from about the same spot in front of the hotel. One hundred and ninety two homes were affected by the tornado and of this number 63 were completely destroyed. Besides this, there were several business places and the elementary school building that were destroyed. Property loss estimated at about $4 million. Nine were killed and 72 injured. As tornadoes go, it is said to have been much slower moving than most, as it took about 25 minutes to go the 16 or 18 blocks through town.

Observers tell of seeing railroad boxcars, whole trees, roofs of buildings and autos, 100 feet up in the air, and of hearing a loud roar like that made by several freight trains.

Elm trees four feet in diameter were uprooted or twisted like toothpicks. Iron beams weighing two tons were carried through the air over one half of a mile. There was some hail and rain before the funnel appeared, but after it had passed the street was completely dry just like a giant vacuum sweeper had come through and dried all of the moisture up.

The people in my picture had been in the basement of the hotel with us and were coming back toward the hotel just as the picture was taken, as they thought the tornado was turning and coming back again. It broke the hotel windows but this was mostly from the flying debris.

Mr. and Mrs. Kermit Christianson

Home Gone

On the farthest southwest corner of Greenwood, probably the first one of the Greenwood homes to be demolished, was that of Ira and Nell Alexander. This had been their home for 39 years.

Nell said, "We heard the whistle. Dale, our son, is a fireman so I looked out to see if the fire was in the neighborhood. It was just a habit. I saw one of the Triplett boys pointing west. They were across the road north. I looked out and there it was almost to us. My brother, Buck, was with us, and we all went into the basement. We looked at the funnel first. We stayed in the basement until it was all over. We didn't hear a roar, just CRACK, CRACK, CRACK!

I could see lights outside so I said, 'There goes my kitchen!' When we came up we thought it was coming back. We couldn't find our dog, Bullet. We took him with us in the basement but he took off. The next day Kenny Weaver and Kelly Alexander were on the Greentown road and they found him.

People came and Dale took us back to town. We stayed overnight with Beierman's because Dale's house had been damaged, too. We picked up some things but most all was gone. The Red Cross and everybody was so good."

Remains of Alexander Home

Mr. and Mrs. Alexander

Cousins Give Accounts

Earl (Buck) Greenman is a farmer who lived all of his life on a farm located eight miles southwest of Tracy. Lots of people know him because he is one of the best fishermen in this part of the country.

On the evening of the storm, he was visiting with his sister and her husband, Mr. and Mrs. Ira Alexander, in Greenwood, and he tells of the experience.

"Nell knew that a tornado had been predicted, but I didn't know anything about it. We heard the siren, but we thought at first it was a fire. Then Nell looked out of the window and said, 'There it is!' I said, 'I want to see that!' I thought it was a fire. I went to look and at first I thought a train was coming down the rail-road track. I saw black dirt on the ground, and watched it for about two minutes, then I dove for the basement.

Nell and Ira were already in the basement. It sounded like a freight train. A lot of the dust blew in the basement. When it started, Nell said, 'There goes my kitchen!'

We waited a few minutes to go up and when we went up the funnel cloud looked like it was by the schoolhouse. Then I looked around for my car. There it was a block away with its' wheels in the air! It was a total wreck. The Alexander's house was all gone except the floor was still there."

At the same time, Earl's cousin, Clyde, was working in a field at the Dale Scott farm southwest of Tracy. He said, "I went to the house and helped the Scott family to the basement. Then I followed the tornado to town.

I got to John Moon's place, one half mile west of town and had to wait for two wagon boxes, a manure spreader and a side delivery rake to get out of the way. It was right ahead of me. A great many cars were hurrying out of town, but I kept on going to the corner south of Greenwood.

I saw my cousin's house explode in the air, another cousins's car wrecked upside down. I went to Dale's (another cousin) and they were hanging blankets over their broken windows. Their house was damaged, but nobody was hurt."

Earl Greenman   Clyde Greenman

Prayed For Safety

Della Daniels Acasio lives in Broadacres, a suburb of Tracy to the south, and located east of the hard hit Greenwood suburb. Her home was not damaged. She was at home when the tornado hit Tracy, and she observed the funnel.

"We didn't know that there were storm warnings out", she said. "It hailed, then it was calm. I walked out in the yard and picked up some hailstones and put them in my deepfreeze because they were as big as pullets' eggs.

Then the fire whistle blew, but I thought it must be a fire. Archie, my son, thought it was a tornado off in the distance so he grabbed his camera.

We looked out and there it was coming right at us. We went in to the basement and began to pray. Then the funnel turned and went downtown, so we came up and watched it for awhile.

We then went to see if Betty (her daughter) and Shirley (a daughter-in-law) were alright, then over to Greenwood. When we got to Nell's (her sister) I could see her white head so I knew she was alright. But her house was gone."

Della Daniels Acasio

21

This is the silhouette of the funnel as seen by Archie Daniels near his home.

Notes Straight From the Hospital

"It was terrible!" said Esther Halverson, well-known nurse here for 26 years. "I was working the 3 – 11 shift with three other nurses. We watched the cloud come, and it looked like it would come directly our way when in turned just enough to miss the hospital. When I saw that I told the other nurses, 'It isn't going to take us but we must get busy and be waiting!'

It wasn't long before people were being brought in, the first one being Mrs. Josephine Sweeley. She was taken to a room per w/c, not hurt, just shaken up and a heart condition.

From that time on, we lost all track of time, as people came in on boards, by wheelchairs, carried in and some walking with help, moaning, crying and bleeding, many in a daze. Our nursing staff was soon there with doctors and nurses from surrounding towns, even a dentist from Walnut Grove and a Tracy veterinarian came to help. Everyone worked.

Soon, relatives started to come hunting for their loved ones, but we worked on, short of water and lights dim, as all was cut off by the storm.

At 3:00 A.M., the regular 3 – 11 shift was sent home to rest, dirty and tired. When I came into my dark house, I felt as though I was one who could and did say, 'Thank You.'

I went to work at 3:00 P.M. again. Things were still crowded

Esther Halverson

23

and extra beds in every corner. Thanks to Miss Wright everything was under control. Again I say it was a terrible experience, something I hope don't ever happen again!"

A visitor at the hospital at the time was Mrs. Joe Johnson, who lived on Emory Street. She said, "We were at the hospital visiting our daughter, Judy. We watched the funnel from the hospital window.

While we were there, one of our neighbors came in in a wheelchair all muddy and dirty. She wasn't hurt bad. She was looking for her little girl because she couldn't find her. But the little girl was found safe. She must have been at a neighbors'.

Other people came in the hospital too, but you couldn't tell who they were because they were so muddy and dirty.

When we got home, just the shell was left of our house. Most of the furniture was still there, but it was so dirty that we had to have it cleaned. We also lost our car and garage."

NOTE: the Johnsons now live 7 ½ miles south of Tracy.

Took Home With Man In It

Mr. and Mrs. Carl Stoltenberg lived in Greenwood, the hardest hit area of the storm center. Mrs. Stoltenberg was fortunately at her son, John's, when the storm hit. Mr. Stoltenberg was in the porch of his home. He said, "I could see boards going by. Then it took my house with me in it and I found myself hurt in a pile of wood somewhere. A boy came along and asked me if I needed help. I said, 'yes" and someone laid me out on the lawn. Then the National Guard came and took me to the hospital. My head was hurt bad and my kidneys were injured."

Fred Stoltenberg, a son of Carl's, also lived in Tracy with his wife and children. He spoke of the storm. "We were watching TV. 'By golly,' I said, 'We are going to get something out of this!'

Just then the fire whistle blew and we went into the basement. We knew what the whistle blew for. The storm put a big rock right through our window. It shoved straws through trees and drain pipes. It blew weeds right through tires. Boy, I know I never want to see another one!"

Carl Stoltenberg

Mr. and Mrs. Fred Stoltenberg

25

Lost Mother, Home and Business

The following was told by Bill and Helen Haney, who lost a Mother, their home, and business in the tornado.

"On June 13 I spent the afternoon weeding and cultivating my garden. After supper it began to look like rain and then around 15 to 7 in started to rain, then some hail came down and I said, 'I suppose my garden will be hailed out after I had worked so hard to get it clean.'

By that time the siren began to blow, so my husband went outside as we thought at first it was a fire whistle. He then called and said, 'Come outside and see what a tornado looks like.' I went outside and could see nothing up there but a big roll of black clouds, dust, wind, and debris. It was coming from the southwest real close. We ran down into the basement and I moved a little steam engine my husband had made away from the northwest corner of the basement, but he made me go over to the southwest corner as he said that was the safest.

Pretty soon the house started to creak and the foundation to crumble. Then there was a 'woosh' as the house flew into the air. We ducked our heads under the piece of canvas my husband had picked up and I didn't know the furnace had fallen against him when the house went, until afterwards.

There was a large section of the cement foundation that had fallen where I had first wanted to sit. We then stood up and watched the tornado go uptown. It was white on the back side.

Then we climbed out and we heard the neighbor lady, Loraine Reiter, across the street, screaming. We could see her head sticking up out of the basement as their floor was still on, and we thought she was pinned there, so we rushed over, but she was just hysterical at what had happened. She clung to us.

We were anxious to go a block and a half down the street to see if we could find my husband's mother, as we could see that her home, as well as all the rest around there, was gone. We looked all over.

Just as I was going past the corner one block east of us, I saw the little girl lying dead on the road and some men carrying someone. Her face was battered, so at first I didn't know who she was, but later I learned she was Mrs. Jeske.

When I got up to Mr. and Mrs. Charles Harnden's yard, there was Millie Harnden lying on a mattress and Charles standing by with his face cut. Millie looked awful and she died when they got her to the hospital. They lived next door to my mother-in-law, Ella Haney, whom my husband found under the divan, after searching all over for her. She was dead.

The authorities called us all to a corner to register so they could find out who was missing. Then we heard that they had found Barbra Holbrook dead in the field just south of Greenwood.

We were afraid of where we were stepping because of electric wires down all over. Then word came that the electricity had been shut off.

Then the people started coming to see if their relatives or friends were alright. Also, some of the neighbors who were gone for the evening or working. The tornado went northeast until it struck the train, then it turned more to the north and took houses and my husband, Bill's shop that was up on Morgan Street.

When we came up out of the basement all we had left was what we had on and our lots where the buildings stood. Bill was hurt some where the furnace had struck him in the side where he had just had an operation six weeks before. Our daughter, Kay, took him to the hospital in their car when they got over here. He had to stay overnight until afternoon next day.

We did not learn the shop was gone until next forenoon when Marvin Wendorf came out and told us that bulldozers and trucks were starting to haul the mashed building away before we could salvage any of our tools or equipment that wasn't broken.

Both our cars were blown over in the park and one was in the trees at Arlo Aiemke's place. They were beyond fixing.

Our daughter and son-in-law, Mr. and Mrs. Harold Radke, took us home with them and we stayed with them for four months until we had another house built. All of our furniture and every bit of our belongings were gone. It is funny where it all could have disappeared to.

The next morning after the tornado we heard that a Mr. Swanson, two blocks from us, was killed, too, and a Paul Swanson was sucked out of his car and killed. There were nine in all that were killed. It was a horrible sight.

One of our little grandson's pictures was found in Minneapolis and a picture of Ella Haney and her husband, Dan, was found at Northfield, Minn. A wedding picture of a cousin of Bill's was found up by Milroy and someone recognized one of the attendants and gave it to them. The cousin was married to Mrs. DeSmits' brother.

Our son-in-law, Harold, found Bill's wrist watch in the middle of the park.

Our other daughter in Cedar Rapids, tried to call and see how we were but couldn't get a call through. Bill's brother and family of Marshall came as soon as they'd heard the news because Mrs. Joe Haney's mother lived here in Greenwood. She was hurt some but mostly shock. They sent their son back to Marshall to make a phone call to relatives to tell them about Ella Haney and that we were OK.

The next day after the tornado we started going through the rubble to find what was left that could be used. We alsso had to make arrangements for the funeral. The churches and people started bringing food and clothing and so many people were so good to us. You just can't believe there are so many good people until something like this strikes. People from Cedar Rapids sent food and clothes along with our daughter, Sharlene, when she and her family came on Saturday. The tornado night 38 people were at Kay and Harold's house most of the night and their electricity and water was shut off so Harold got some water and took it out to Ovie Gullickson's restaurant and cooked up a big pot of coffee for us, and Harold got the Gamble Store owner to open up and sell him a gas lantern so we would have lights. I hope we never have to live through anything like that again."

The Holden Family

Standing in the beautiful bright sunshine on their lawn, Bud and Iona Holden and their son, Brad, saw the then bluish grey funnel cloud about four miles from their home on the southeast edge of Garvin.

The funnel rose higher and higher, and it was very large around. Something white seemed to be whirling around outside of the funnel as it went northeast, disappearing after it took the Glen Horsman farm. Then as it took the Charles Carter farm they saw it again.

Mrs Holden recalled that a man saw down into the "eye" or "heart" of the funnel. This is a rare experience. It has been said that the inside of the funnel becomes lighted by lightning flashes, which makes it a beautiful, though frightful sight. Certainly it is an experience not had by many.

The Tracy Tornado As I Remember It

Pam Haugen was eight years old in 1968, but she can still well remember her once in a lifetime experience. She wrote the following essay especially for this book.

"It was ten to seven and I was at Linda's house (Linda is Pam's older sister). I was sitting on the table watching the hail balls. I asked Linda if we should go in the basement. She said we would if it got bad enough. Linda was writing a letter to her husband who was in Washington in the service.

We sat there for a while, then Linda wanted to go and see if the hailstones were hurting her car. When we looked out of the window a siren blew but we just thought it was a fire whistle. Then we saw the tops of the weeping willow bending over and touching the ground. Linda said we better go in the basement so we went and got Nancy (her little girl who was sleeping) and started for the basement. When we were in the living room I heard the picture window break. We were starting down the basement steps when the door blew open and pulled us out!

The last I saw of Linda until after the storm was her rolling around on the grass. Then the tornado picked me up and carried me a block away. It was like boards and nails would come toward me but they would go right through me.

I remember seeing a man coming up from his basement. But just then the tornado picked me up and took me back to Linda's house (what was left of it).

When It was over, I saw two men carrying Linda. They told me to follow them, but all I did was stand there and scream.

My brother was driving through Greentown to see if we were ok. I hollered to Chuck but he didn't know who I was. I told him I was Pam, his little sister. He picked me up and put me in his car. As we were leaving a man asked Chuck to send an ambulance out here right away.

Chuck took me home. Mom was getting into the car to come and see if Linda and Nancy and I were alright. But when she saw me she jumped in the car and took me to the hospital.

A day or so after being in the hospital, I received word that Linda was ok, but that Nancy was dead."

Pam Haugen

A Child is Dead

Love never dies, and none knows this better than Linda Vaske, one of the critically injured by the tornado. Her love and kindness to little two year old Nancy Ann Vlahos will live forever, though the little girl was swept out of Linda's arms by the ravaging wind, and killed. She was the youngest victim of the storm.

Linda and her husband were waiting for the day when they could adopt the pretty little girl who made her home with them. Linda's husband, Clifford, was at basic training at Ft. Lewis, Washington, at the time of the storm. He could hardly believe it when he heard the news.

Apparently, Linda held the little girl tightly but the force of the wind tore her from Linda's arms and into the street. Linda was rolling around on the ground in the front of their house. She couldn't get up off the ground and looked around screaming for the child.

Linda was suffering from deep gashes on both legs and on her head. She was bleeding so badly when friends rushed her into a car to the hospital that every minute counted. Never thinking of herself, her only concern was for little Nancy.

Linda and Nancy

32

The Pool Family

John and Betty Pool and their four children lived in Broadacres. Betty said, "We were eating supper. We hadn't heard any warnings. It started to rain real hard and then it hailed. I looked out of the window and said to John, 'You won't have any garden left if this keeps on!'

The whistle started to blow. I came in the living room and looked out of the window and there was a great big cloud in the sky. John looked out and said, 'Go in the basement!' I stayed there with the kids and John looked out of the window, then he came back down and the lights went out.

We stayed there for a while in the darkness, then came up and saw the funnel cloud whirling in the sky in the northeast part of town. It was the funniest feeling. You never saw anything like it in your life.

We didn't even know that it had already hit, but John said, 'Let's go over to Greenwood.' (His folks lived there.) We went over there and got to the Greenwood road and there stood John's mother, all covered with dirt, walking. She said that his dad had gotten cut badly.

She told John to 'take the family home.' So we came home and John and his mother went back to her home, which was completely demolished. Someone had treated his dad's hand, which had been cut on a fruit jar."

John Pool family

The Alexander family

Elva Alexander and her husband, Jonas, lived at 118 2^(nd) Street. Although their home wasn't hit by the tornado, they lived only two blocks east of its' path.

"I said to my husband, Jonas, 'Let's go into the basement!' He wanted to watch out of the front door at it hailing so hard. Then he said 'It looks bad. Let's go down to the basement now.' I heard the telephone ring so I ran up to answer it, but no one said anything.

I just got back down when I heard a noise like a million jets going over, and the wind was blowing so hard I wanted to run up and close the back door that I had left open in case of the storm. It was on the north side of our house. My husband said, 'no, don't go up.'

It was over in ten minutes, so I waited then went up to look out of the front door of our house. Everyone was running up to the end of our block. So I went to see. I saw two blocks up west.

Four of five boxcars from the railroad were on Morgan Street, and there were big trees in the street.

Soon, my brother, Frank Greenman, came from the roundhouse, where he works. He was all dirt and his head was bleeding, but not badly. He was stunned and shaking, but alive, anyway. Then he went back to the roundhouse. A lot of other people and myself watched until dark. We saw them take dead people with blankets over them, to the hospital. They took them in trucks.

My brother said he was told by the boss at the roundhouse to put the big door down but to leave it open a foot at the bottom. He looked through it and he saw Greenwood all up in the air.

He got in the southwest part and would have lain down but he was afraid it would cover him up. So he stood up all of the time. He was hit three times in the head. If it had hit him again he knew that it would have killed him. He had pieces of shingles in his shirt pocket.

I went down to the roundhouse the next day, and the Lord was with my brother, because that whole east pit was filled with wire and cars and tin just packed full, just room enough left for Frank.

Frank Greenman & Elva Alexander

There was a big freight train just pulled into town and it Tipped every boxcar on it over, and they were filled with stone.

The men all ran to the depot and so did all the help at the roundhouse except for Frank, who didn't have time after the boss told him to put the big door down on the west side. Only Frank's cap blew away."

A car came in and landed beside Frank Greenman in the pit here.

Florence Smith

Florence Smith lived in Greenwood, but she was downtown at Shirley's café, where she worked, at the time the storm hit. Her words reflect the horror of that night.

"About the time that the whistle blew Jack Holbrook came into the café and told us that there was a tornado between the railroad track and the café. He told us to go for a cellar, but there wasn't any cellar there.

We watched out of the back side door until the bricks from the hotel started coming at the café. I was holding on to Vicki Strand, Shirley's daughter. We crawled under the booths.

There were about nineteen people in the café. They all crawled under the booths for protection. We saw a tree coming and we watched it. It went into the roof of Bill Johnson's grocery store next door.

After it was all over we looked around. There was a tree across the back door of the café so we couldn't get out. We moved the tree so we could get the back door open. People were running like crazy.

I decided to go home. When I got out to where the old town pump used to be, I didn't know where I was at. You just could not tell. I couldn't see where the road was because there was so much debris and all.

When I got down where my daughter, Harriet, lived, I saw a baby. It was dead. Someone asked me if I could identify it, if it was my granddaughter. I couldn't identify the baby. Then I saw Harriet and the three children coming down the road so I knew that they were alright.

Then I went down to where I lived. I couldn't tell exactly where I lived. Our house

Florence Smith

36

was mostly demolished. I began to look around to see if I could find anybody. Ed, my husband, was at the high school, but he came out to help.

Our cat disappeared, but returned about six months later. He had been hurt."

Sadie Van Dusen

Mrs. Sadie Van Dusen of 803 North Third Street spent two months in the Tracy Municipal Hospital. Her smile reflects her thankfulness to be alive after an encounter close to the "valley of death."

"I didn't hear the storm warnings," she said. "I looked out of the window and saw big hailstones fall. They were as big as golf balls. I got some of them and put them in my refrigerator, then went outside again.

It was blowing pretty hard. I tried to get to the neighbor's house but I thought the front door was locked. It must have been the suction.

I looked across the street to the Postmaster's house. We did not have a basement in the house. Everything, boards and trees, were coming down the road.

I don't remember anything then. I thought I better get in my own house, but the back door kept hitting me in the face, and hitting me again and again. Then when the storm took the house I was on the back steps. It pulled me over the foundation. If it was another minute, I'd have been in the house and went with it."

She continued slowly, "As soon as it was over, my neighbors all looked around. 'The sun came out real pretty', they said.

They said that they saw me but they thought it was a stump on the step. Some thought it was a dog. I crawled out, but I don't remember it.

They got me in the back of a truck and took me to the hospital. I said to one of my neighbors, 'Oh Carl, my chest hurts,' but I don't remember it. At the hospital they later told me that I had said to someone, 'go see how my neighbors are. Go see how Paul is.' They found Paul dead in my rock garden. He had lived in one of my cabins. I had ten cabins and they were all gone."

Mrs. Van Dusen talked calmly now. "Some people were heard to say, 'All I have left are the clothes on my back.' But for me, I didn't even have my clothes left, because they had to cut them off at the hospital.

It took them three hours to get the ground pebbles out of me and to clean me up. I had three broken ribs, a broken wind-pipe, a collapsed left lung, a right lung full of blood, and a deep gash in my head."

Mrs. Van Dusen had her new home built exactly like the one that the tornado destroyed, because she "liked that one so well"

Mrs. Van Dusen

Home of Mrs. Van Dusen after tornado

Mrs. Van Dusen and new home at 803 N. Third St.

Former Carver farm located southwest of Tracy one of the first to be in twister's path. This photo taken several months later.

Trees that had stood for many years so beautiful through the seasons, now are torn and shredded and twisted, many uprooted by the great force of the wind.

We Have To Get Through

In my home at Chandler, Minnesota, on the evening of June 13, I little knew that in my hometown less than 40 miles away, tragedy had struck. There were friends visiting at my house, and we were listening to stereo music, never guessing that the dark clouds outside would do so much damage.

Early the next morning someone called from the Air Force Base and said, "Did you know that a tornado hit Tracy last night?" I was astonished. My family lives there.

"It can't be bad." I kept telling myself, but quickly I got the children up and rushed them into the car. We stopped at a friend's house and she drove us to Tracy.

We had to stop at the Garvin Corner to get oil in the car, so I asked the man there if it was true and how bad it was. He said, "yes, it is true. It's really a mess. There are people dead and a lot more are hurt. It hit the south suburb worst." My heart nearly stopped. The south suburb is where my mother and brothers and sister and their families all live. Oh no! What if? But, then I couldn't think clearly anymore. I bowed my head and prayed.

We arrived at the east entrance of the city only to be met by several National Guardsmen. They stopped us and informed us that we couldn't get into Tracy. "But we have to get through," we cried, "Our family is there. They may need help!" One of the men nodded to the other and said to us, "Go over there and get a pass first." He piped up as we started to leave with, "Hope they're alright." How comforting.

We went to get the pass, where we met Mr. and Mrs. Marlow Nelson of Balaton. Mrs. Nelson told me that my family was safe, but that Aunt Nell had lost her home and her belongings.

We made the rest of the trip, unbelieving the terrible sights that we saw, to meet each family member to assure us of their safety. "Oh thank God!" And the tears came, for joy that they were safe, and for sadness for all who were not.

And There Were Freakish Sights

- A tree uprooted and then replanted through the roof of a house.
- Railroad tracks turned in different directions as their steel took a new form.
- A carp fish from Lake Sarah, the funnel's beginning sight, was carried to Tracy and then deposited in a tree.
- Animals and pets mysteriously disappeared, then suddenly came back to the spot that was once their home, some as long as several months later.
- A huge boxcar was taken from the tracks and stripped, then set down blocks away.
- Bank checks, photographs, and other papers were found in the Minneapolis area; being carried by the funnel over 150 miles away.
- The north wall of a home in north Tracy was completely taken away, exposing the stairway and the entire home's interior to the passerby.

It was written in the book of Matthew in the twenty-fourth chapter, verse thirty five, "Heaven and Earth shall pass away, but My words shall not pass away." A stranger walked through the rubble that remained after the storm and he came upon an open Bible. Next to it were bits of ruined wood and broken bricks and clothing torn to shreds. The house that once stood there was gone, and the once lovely trees were now bare fragments of roots.

Not far away, bodies were found and other people had been injured. It looked as if the earth, here, had truly "passed away."

Perhaps this opened book, most beloved and most read of all books, was left to comfort those who had lost their loved ones, and for courage for those whose homes were gone beyond repair. Or perhaps its' words were visible proof of His greatness.

People asked, "why", as question no mortal man can answer, asked by those hurt so deeply that their wounds of heart would seem to be beyond healing power.

Yet, John 14:18 bears the words of One who suffered still more, "I will not leave you comfortless. I will come to you."

A Glimpse Of The Past

Disaster is not new to Tracy. However, the 1968 tornado was the worst in it's history.

Back in 1891, while Tracy was but sixteen years old, a great destructive fire swept through the then call "village" in November. This fire destroyed twenty six buildings and did damage of an estimated $50,000.00.

In 1940, an early spring fire in the Tracy Hotel did much damage to the hotel, as well as injuring several people who tried to jump from the upper stories.

In 1960, another fire raged through the Central Stockyards, and burned many cattle to death.

Still another downtown fire in 1956 destroyed some of the stores down on Main Street, and damaged others.

Then the tornado of 1924 did damage mostly to farm places, although a young Tracy farmer was killed in this storm, and the baby he held and protected, was spared.

Thus it seems this small city has suffered beyond what one could imagine. Yet, always it has come through disaster exceptionally well.

Facts About The Tracy Tornado

- For eleven miles the tornado touched the ground.
- Recording equipment in Tracy was damaged by the tornadic winds and rain.
- For 72 hours people worked and searched for dead and injured.
- One hundred sixty men in the National Guard were called to help.
- Telephone lines, electric lines, and water and gas supplies were cut off.
- The same night as the Tracy tornado, there was one at Lake Okoboji, Iowa.
- Many homes had to have "condemned" signs put on them, as they were found unsafe for people to enter or to live in.
- The Red Cross and other such organizations came to feed the homeless, supply clothing and shelter.
- The warning alert saved many other lives, as upon hearing it many people went into their basements.
- At least a block wide strip of residential area was completely wiped out, although great damage was done for several blocks wide.
- Four farms were completely wiped out.
- The funnel was said to have deposited its' "catch" of fish from Lake Sarah, in Tracy, seemingly making room for all it picked up in Tracy to carry for miles away again.
- Several people reported that their farms had been hit for the second time by tornadic winds; proof that there is truth in the old saying that "history repeats itself", see 1924 tornado.
- Probably more good, clear photographs were taken of this funnel at close range than of any other one known.
- Most of the dead victims lived in the Greenwood area.

This was the new part of the grade school. Most of the windows were broken and the damage was great. The old part of the building was completely crumbled; some said that it looked as if it has been bombed

Hospital Spared

Fortunately spared from destruction was the new Municipal Hospital in the far east section of the city. Here the injured were taken for treatment, some for severe injuries that would take months to heal, others for puncture wounds that could be treated on an out-patient basis.

The ground in dirt that overly covered those brought in, took hours to clean off. The dead were not easily identified as they were piled in the hospital's laundry room until relatives or friends could come to claim their own. There was crying and sobbing as the shocked survivors came in. Mass sorrow, it was, for many in such a small city knew all of the dead and injured.

There was no rest for those who had the duties there to tend to the injured or to lend a word of comfort to the bereaved. In time help would come from other towns, but in these first moments it was a trying time for all.

There was a bright moment in a dark night when a near-hysterical mother found her lost child to be alive and safe with a neighbor.

Every story was not bright, however. A little girl was killed when the tornadic wind whisked her out of the arms of the woman who loved this child as her very own, and who planned to adopt her. The woman herself was injured very critically when she was swept into the air and down again.

The following information is condensed from "The Bulletin" a St. Louis Park Medical Center publication, by the courtesy of Dr. Norman Lee, physician in charge the night of the tornado. He took pictures of the approaching tornado, as well as movies of the storm. These were used by Walter Cronkite on his CBS program.

Dr. Lee recalls the terrifying high pitched constant whine of the siren intermingled with the roar of the on-coming tornado. When the electrical power went off and the siren stopped, he felt an odd personal sense of abandonment by civilization. Dr. Lee went directly to the hospital as soon as the storm had passed. His own home was not damaged.

"Most of the injured who did not survive the tornado were killed outright. The majority of the patients had numerous wounds from flying glass. Many had abrasions and contusions from falling objects, and there were some burns. Approximately 20 percent of the patients had orthopedic injuries. The skin of most of the patients was black from dirt and many had been tattooed with dirt. One patient developed tetanus.

All patients were sent to the Municipal Hospital. They came in ambulances, on stretchers, and on makeshift stretchers of doors and boards. The dead were placed in the hospital laundry room which was used as a temporary morgue. Tags signed by the physician. Tetanus toxoid shots were given almost routinely to patients who entered the emergency room. The following day the county health nurse gave tetanus boosters at the Municipal building to a large number of the townspeople.

Cots, beds and supplies were sent to the hospital from the Christian Manor Nursing Home and from Tracy, Incorporated, both 60 bed nursing homes. These were placed in the corridors and patient rooms. The solarium, lobby and dining rooms were also used for patients whose care could not be delayed. Some of these had their lacerations sutured the following day. Only one patient had major surgery done the first evening.

Although the hospital proper had auxiliary generators for electricity, the emergency room did not; consequently two generators were brought from adjacent towns. Because many patients brought in were coated with dirt the nursing and volunteer personnel contributed significantly by washing and cleaning up the wounds. Fortunately none of the physicians in town was injured and none of the medical facilities of Tracy was affected by the tornado.

Two years previous to the tornado a bus-truck accident had occurred six miles west of Tracy. At that time 41 teenagers were injured and two died. The medical staff had learned much from that experience about handling mass casualties, and that knowledge was an important factor in the successful management of the tornado disaster.

Dr. Lee noted an interesting observation that approximately one week following the tornado he began to see patients for a severe dry bronchitis cough and chest discomfort. The cough became productive and the secretions were tarry black. He estimated that 40 – 50 patients were seen by him for this type of respiratory distress. Approximately six developed bronchopneumonia. It is presumed that particulate matter inhaled during the storm caused this unusual condition.

In the final analysis it was the volunteers, the professionals, and nonprofessionals, all the people with a helping hand and a willing heart who provided the compassion and talents necessary for adequate emergency and disaster care.

The following list of physicians gave unselfishly of their time and talents during and following the tornado:

- Dr. Norman J. Lee, Tracy
- Dr. P. Bosley, Balaton,
- Dr. R.O. Schroeppel, Tracy
- Dr. W.G. Workman, Tracy
- Dr. C.W. Graham, a radiologist from Spirit Lake, Iowa who flew in the night of the tornado
- Dr. J.B. Sawyer, a dentist from Walnut Grove
- Dr. E.K. Bicek, a veterinarian from Tracy who also assisted

Volunteer doctors were:

- Dr. J.E. Eckdale, Marshall
- Dr. K.A. Peterson, Marshall
- Dr. R.W. Taintor, Marshall
- Dr. P.C. Hedenstrom, Marshall
- Dr J.E. Bader, Slayton
- Dr. R.F. Pierson, Slayton
- Dr. H Patterson, Slayton
- Dr. Nywall, Slayton
- Dr. R. Kotval, Pipestone
- Dr. R.W. Keyes, Pipestone

The wind, like a chained monster, suddenly let loose, did its' wicked damage and then left the scene as suddenly as it had come. The injured were thankful for those who were spared to care for them. Nurses and doctors did a great job.

This gleaming hospital, equipped with the newest and best for caring for the injured victims of the tornado, was a busy thoroughfare. For some, it was a short trip for minor injuries; but for others, it became their home for months to come.

Roll Of The Dead

1. Mrs. Charles Harnden, age 75, was found dead in front of her home in Greenwood after the tornado. She had lived in the Tracy area for 60 years. Her husband, who was thrown out of the back door of their home, was hospitalized.

2. Mrs. John Werner, age 75, who had lived in Tracy since 1922, was being led to the basement by her husband, when something hit her. Mr. Werner was not seriously injured.

3. Mr. Walter Swanson, age 47, who lived with his brother, Louis in Greenwood, was killed and found in an alley. He was outside when the tornado hit.

4. Mrs. Dan Haney, age 84, was thown from the back door of her home in Greenwood.

5. Fred Pilatus, who had been crippled for five years and used a walker to get around. His wife was also injured.

6. Mrs. Ellen Morgan, age 75, was visiting in the home of Miriom Nelson when the storm hit. The home was demolished and her body was found amongst the ruins.

7. Mrs. Barbara Holbrook, age 50, was a lifelong resident of Tracy. Her body was found about 200 yards from her home which was also demolished. Her family was all safe in the basement.

8. Paul Swanson, in his 60's, was the one occupant of the Van Dusen cabins north of Highway 14, who was killed. His body was found

in a rock garden. The owner of the cabins, Mrs. Sadie Van Dusen, was seriously injured.

9. Nancy Vaske, age 2, was torn from the arms of the young woman who loved her. Linda, who had been mother to little Nancy, was critically injured and her sister, Pam Haugen, was also injured when she was drawn from a window, blown away, then blown back again.

In Memoriam

To the memory of those who will be sadly missed in Tracy; the nine who lost their lives in the tornado:

Their very lives the storm did claim.
And now these markers bear each name.
And June 13 of '68,
the night the victims met with fate.

No time to plan or hardly know
What tragedy life can bestow
Was theirs; the nine whose bodies lie
Beneath the sod, and now clear sky

Bless all who loved them; every one.
And when their life on earth is done,
they shall then join them hand in hand
in one far better, all safe land.

No storm clouds gather anymore.
No funnel swoops, and there no roar
of death comes suddenly at night
to snuff out life like candle light!

Other Tornado Disasters

Feb. 19, 1884: A series of about 60 tornadoes east and south of Illinois and Kentucky took around 800 lives, and destroyed more than 10,000 buildings.

March 18, 1925: A series of tornadoes in Illinois, Indiana, Kentucky, Tennessee and Missouri killed 830, left 13,000 injured and 15,000 homeless. There were 35 towns damaged heavily. Property loss was $18,000,000.

April 2, 1936: A twister killed 400 in Mississippi and Georgia and injured 2,000.

Jan. 30, 1947: Tornadoes in Texas and Oklahoma killed 138 and injured 1300.

March 22, 23, 1952: Tornadoes in Arkansas and neighboring states killed 236 people.

May and June, 1953: Tornadoes killed 124 in Texas, 116 in Michigan, and 90 in Massachusetts.

June 23, 1962: A killing twister in the southern suburbs of Chicago caused $1 million damage.

April 3, 1964: At Wichita Falls, Texas, 7 lost their lives and $15 million damages.

Oct. 3, 1964: At Larose, La., 21 were killed and 1752 injured in a twister there.

Some Interesting Facts About Tornadoes

- Likened to an elephant's trunk, a tornado often sways back and forth sucking up water or whatever is in its' path.
- Tornadoes are rare in mountainous area and in most of the foreign countries.
- May and June are the most likely months for tornadoes to hit, and the hours they are most likely to hit are between three and seven P.M.
- Tornadoes may strike the same target more than once. In 1916, 1917, and 1918, and always on May 20, tornadoes hit Codell, Kansas.
- Snow has even been dumped from a funnel cloud.
- Most generally rain or hail preceded most tornadoes.
- Sometimes the winds have reached 500 m.p.h. during a storm.
- Sometimes one home is broken to bits, while the one next to it is left unharmed.
- Tornadoes have been known to drive straw into steel.
- People can be hurled through the air and deposited safely on the ground again.
- Some who have observed a tornado, report a strong, gassy odor accompanying the funnel.
- Many smaller funnels may project from the mother storm.
- Alaska, Nevada, and Rhode Island are the safest states, as seldom does a tornado strike there.
- Homes have been seen to be torn from their foundations and into the air, where they may explode.
- There have been various sounds with tornadic winds, some of which have been described as "hissing, screaming, cracking, and roaring."

Characteristics Of Tornado Weather And Explanations

The usual color of tornado clouds is a greenish black. The clouds come from the southwest and they seem to be angrily boiling and churning downward. The air may be calm and humid and may have an odor similar to gas that makes it hard to breathe as the funnel nears the ground.

It is theorized that shock wave intersections cause the actual tornado. When the shock wave bypasses the cold front, the air pressure rises sharply.

The explosions of buildings that are often described, are caused by the force of the wind currents, which cause a vacuum at the center of the whirling mass.

The funnel may be thin and rope like, small in diameter, or wide and thick like a huge funnel itself. The inside is made up of rolling clouds, with or without lightning.

Although many people have the opinion that tornadoes appear only in the hotter months of June or July, it is not always the case. During the month of February, 1971, for instance, 130 people were killed in a twister and 121 of these were killed within four hours of the 21st of February, when one tornado was on the ground for 121 miles from Cary, Miss. To Middleton, Tennessee. The air during this particular month of February was said to be unusually warm and humid.

Descriptions of the noise made when the funnel touches the ground are numerous. Some liken it to a giant vacuum sweeper, to freight trains, roaring airplanes, buzzing of bees, and hissing sounds. The pressure seems to build up in people's heads, making one feel as if his head were to "pop open."

Hurricanes and earthquakes have done much damage, as storms go, but none can compete with the tornado.

"The clouds poured out water: the skies sent out a sound: thine arrows also went abroad. The voice of thy thunder was in the heaven: the lightnings lightened the world: the earth trembled and shook." PSALM 77:17, 18

The Tornado Of 1924

It was late on a Sunday afternoon, June 23, 1924. A funnel formed at Lake Benton and before it came to the end of its' journey at Lamberton, it had done a million dollars damage, killed three people, and left 37 families homeless. Most of the damage was done to farm places.

One of the victims was a farmer who lived four miles west of Tracy, john Edwards. All of his farm buildings were demolished and the 14 other people in the house at the time of the storm were injured, some hospitalized in serious condition.

This funnel was said by those who recall it to have travelled fast, probably at about the rate of 60 m.p.h. Along with its' violent wind came a very heavy rainfall, and there was a one half to one mile wide country stretch and a 60 mile long length of storm center. It came as close as one half mile south of the city limits of Tracy.

The course that this storm followed was zigzag in design. Although it came very close to many towns on its' way, it did not go through the towns themselves.

The one time beautiful farm country was left flattened while many families lost their homes, their belongings, their livestock, and their crops.

Then, too, 45 years ago from the tornado of 1968, kind neighbors and friends came in to clean up and rebuild once more what had been destroyed after so many years of gathering together.

These are examples of the damage done to the homes that were in the path of the twister. Many, like these, had to be torn down.

Most unusual of sights to anyone driving down Highway 14 is north Tracy, was this house, with one entire side taken off. The house could be likened to a giant "doll house." Note the stairway still intact.

Hundreds of residents lost their cars in the storm. Many were hurled into the air and then thrown down blocks away. The great force of the tornadic winds crushed this semi-trailer. It could well have been mistaken for a highway accident.

This building was once the Clinic Hospital. Several years ago a new Municipal Hospital was built in the eastern section of the city and this old building was sold to be used for a home. The new Municipal Hospital was fortunately spared of damage by the storm.

This section of Greenwood, once covered with homes, now has a few new homes built where the old ones were blown away.

Residential Area

In Case Of A Tornado

1. Open a window or a door on the opposite side of the storm's direction, usually the north and east sides.

2. Leave a radio or television on to listen for reports from the U.S. Weather Bureau.

3. Have flashlights ready.

4. Don't touch dangling wires.

5. Store as many loose items as possible underground.

6. Know your warning alert system, and be able to distinguish the siren from other sirens.

7. Stay in the basement or storm cellar long enough. People have been killed because they came up to soon.

8. Watch for fires and escaping gas.

9. Be careful for nails after the storm.

10. Keep out of the disaster area unless you are qualified to help. Do not get in the way of emergency vehicles.

11. If possible when in the basement, keep underneath an old table or something else to protect yourself from flying articles.

12. Keep as calm as possible.

Tracy Will Live Again!

Oh ramshacked ruins of despair
I watch you crumbled, partly there
Yet so much gone; and so much grief
We shake our heads in unbelief!

Still and bereaved your people sigh and
mourn, perhaps too deep to cry
For loved ones gone, now lain to rest
Yet midst the ruins stands the test!

Stand stalwart, people, join together
To face the future's brighter weather.
There will be sun again upon this sod
You have assurance from our living God!

From this experience of sadness here
You may be left with grief and even fear
Of days ahead. But face tomorrow great
And stronger bound since nature's cruel fate.

Epilogue

The courageous people of Tracy would not, and did not, let their town die. From neighboring towns and even from far away, people came to help clean up the mess. From there the rebuilding process came. Homes went up fast, and the cleanup crews worked long hours to clear home sights and to beautify the area.

Now the Tracy Tornado is history. The scars that remain are mostly in the hearts of those who lost most, their loved ones, neighbors and friends.

Most of us take for granted at the start of a day that it shall also have an ending. But we are not sure if we will see that end, or if our paths will cross once more with those who are close to us.

Only in the great books, hidden to us here, lies this knowledge. But there at Tracy the people grew closer to one another and their loved ones in a common loss, and there was a tie not to be broken by the stoppage of a clock at 7:04 P.M.

About The Author

Irene Daniels Bakker was born in Tracy on February 28, 1931. She grew up in Tracy, graduating from High School there in 1949.

She has had poetry appearing in the Pageant of Poetry Books, America Sings, and Sermons in Poetry, as well as in newspapers.

She presently lives in the Chanarambie Valley at Chandler, Minnesota. It is her hope that this first book contains the sentiment she feels for her hometown and its' people.

It was unintentional if some were left out of these pages, and the author sincerely thanks all who so willingly cooperated while she was compiling it.

The original book "TORNADO!" was written in 1968, shortly following the tragic tornado in Tracy, Minnesota. This updated book, written in 2011, 43 years later, contains memories that some people who lived in or near Tracy at the time have since recorded about this day. Along with photos of new homes and businesses in Tracy since that time, the writer hopes to show how a people in this southwestern Minnesota town have remembered and gone ahead from those memories to rebuild what material things were lost and remember those people who died that day in the tornado. Here are some of these recordings made years later:

DOUG BENGTSON now at Wood Lake, Mn. Who writes: I remember that day quite well. I lived on a farm southwest of Balaton just to the east of Currant Lake. The day started out like any other day getting up and going off to Vo-Tec in Pipestone. I would get off in the afternoon and then home to help dad with farm work. The day was hot and windy even somewhat muggy but nothing more than that to allow us to think there would be severe weather so close. Most of the weather had passed in the early afternoon and we were in the house eating supper and waiting for dad to come in from doing chores. I don't know what caused him to look off to the east but as he was about half way to the house we could hear him call to us. He was pointing off to the east and we ran out and looked at that funnel hanging there. We were only about 10 or so miles west of where it was. I still remember the width of the tornado as it ran along the ground. It was very wide at the base and black as night. I later learned that when the sun shines on storm clouds it makes them look dark. As we watched it move off to the northeast I said to dad that thing is headed for Tracy. It was not too much later that we heard on the radio that it had hit Tracy. Although we heard reports of tornados falling out of the sky in many other places this one was a sure thing. Later that evening we drove down to see the damage but we could not get very close. It was plain to see however that this twister cut a wide path right through the middle of town. No doubt, the loss of lives was the most tragic thing that happened that day, but I hope I never see one like that again in all my life. My uncle writes in his diary about this tornado. His diary is in the Balaton Library.

JIM MOLINE who now lives in Marshall, Mn. Gave the following account of his memories of that day: I grew up 2 miles west of the Lake

Sarah Baptist church. I was 9 years when the 1968 Tornado occurred. The funnel cloud rotated almost directly over our farm place. Our whole family stood in our yard watching it. My Dad said it was nothing and told me to go to the house and get wash water for milking the cows. I went outside to our front porch and then went out to the front of our yard to see past our grove of trees. That is when I actually saw the tornado come out of the sky. I saw the gray colored tornado right before it hit the inlet on Lake Shetek. I saw the tornado turn from gray to white from the bottom up as it was picking water out of the lake. We ended up following the twister and drove into Tracy shortly after it went through. I remember us driving into Tracy shortly after and it was a mess! We also stopped by a farm place that was leveled near the lake. I can't remember the name of the family. My older brother Jerry was actually doing fieldwork at my grandparents farm about 1/2 to ¾ miles from the tornado touchdown and did not even know what was happening. He just continued cultivating.

VERNON GRINDE, then principal of Tracy Elementary School faced a different kind of devastation but he and his family made it through without injury. "My children were home with me, two boys and two girls, when we heard a tornado was coming they told me "Dad, we will have to go into the basement" Grinde said. The younger children huddled under couch cushions, he said, and I got sort of in the middle of them. Not long after the tornado passed, Grinde and a school janitor rushed to the elementary school, only to find it completely flattened. 'It was an old 1895 building. We had added some things to it, first grade and kindergarten rooms he said. 'It was very ironic there was a room right off my office where we kept all the school records. I checked and they were all still there. They could have been flying around yet "I'll never forget, we had two older ladies who lived next to us" Grinde said. I asked my neighbors about them and they said, "Oh they're all right. They were sitting on their back screened–in porch they said they didn't know there was a storm."

TED SCHOTZKO who still lives by Tracy was out on the delivery route for his business, Lakeland Meats, when he learned of the storm. "I stopped at Kerkaert's store south of Marshall. While I was in the store every ambulance and fire truck around went past, going 90 miles an hour" Schotzko said. Schotzko started home but was stopped on Hwy. 14 by a National Guard roadblock. Chuck DeVetter said "I had to go a half mile north of town and come into town by the airport road." Once he got to the edge of the tornado's path Schotzko had to travel by foot because of the debris. "For the last few blocks I forgot how to say a Hail Mary," he said. It's quite a shock and that was 40 years ago. Schotzko's first wife Lois and four of their 10 children were at home during the tornado. However, they made it to the basement in time, and were unhurt. The tornado left both psychological and physical effects for many survivors. Some say they became more spiritual Schotzko said even with the loss of life there must have been a reason for it all.

LILLIAN ARNE ZAJIC lives in Tyler MN. She said "My folks had a house on Harvey Street. The tornado came across the street southeast and took the garage off the house that was on the west edge and then a brick from the big tall grade school building. The brick turned east and went through the folks house wall on the west side after the garage was off the brick flew across the bathroom bathtub and broke it; hit the toilet stool and broke it so water was all over the bathroom floor. Mother's living room furniture on the south wall was blown across to the north wall. Broken windows put glass all over the carpet. A small yard stick from a Greentown lady was stuck into mother's wall in the living room. The folks' home was pushed a foot off the foundation to north. My daddy Norris Arne had to put block and tackle to pull the house back south on the foundation so the folks got water in the basement from future rains. They put in drain and septic pump for future living. Daddy Norris built this new home in 1948 from basement on up. The folks had a double garage in their back yard but that tornado did not touch the back garage but it took the front house garage off slick and clean from the house wall. Ed Radke home was just east of the folks and not touched on the same block. Glenna Hedger home was to the west of the folks' house and was damaged bad. I, Lillian Arne Zajic was married and living one mile east of Currie, Mn, on Hwy 30. We heard the terrible news over my battery radio and we drove to Tracy to see how the folks were. Mom was at the Tracy Hospital in the basement as a cook for supper. After it was all over with she drove home and got two flat tires on her car and saw her house car garage was gone. She went in the house and saw the glass all over the floor. She started sweeping up the glass on the living room floor. She was fine and glad to see Henry and I. We brought jugs of water and a hot dish. We took boards and boarded up the broken windows. Daddy was up north at Akeley, Mn. He drove home the next day but could hardly find the right street from Hwy. 14 to go to the house. Henry wore a pair of bib overalls and a shirt with a pliers and hammer and he could walk everywhere down town to help for the city would not let any outsider come in town but it was my folks and they welcomed all help

RUSSELL HIVELY who now lives in Neosho, Mo. Wrote about his view of the Tracy tornado like this: "The afternoon was sunny and bright where we were the afternoon of the Tracy tornado. We had heard the weather warnings on the radio and were watchful as we headed out to milk our cows. My wife Kay and son Rusty and I lived northeast of Balaton at the time. A huge sliding barn door opened to the south where we watched the tornado raise havoc southeast of us while I milked our cows. I do not recall who spotted it first, but it was a huge tornado venturing out across the lands. I think there were dark clouds with it and some lightning, still the weather remained pleasant where we watched from. I recall how the spout changed colors as the tornado slowly edged its way on to Tracy. It was coal black like the soil most of the time. A couple times it turned a greenish gray like water would when we water painted in grade school. I continued milking and after a few minutes the destructive tornado disappeared into dark clouds and out of our sight."

BETTY POOL who still lives in Tracy remembers: "It was June 13, 1968, a hot, windy day. That evening Tracy changed! We were sitting at the table eating when the whistles blew! I got up, went to the south window and looked out. There in the sky was a huge black cloud. John said "Go in the basement." I took our four children and went in the basement. This was a day that anyone living in Tracy at the time will never forget! When we hear the whistles blow we look to the sky. We remember that day! We are alert! Yes, Tracy has changed! Nine lives were lost that day. Buildings were destroyed! Many new buildings have been built since then. Many homes have replaced those destroyed. The tornado didn't hit one section of town but came very close. It hit the new foundation of the high school they had just started to build. Later they finished building it. Then it went through the Greenwood area destroying many homes, then up through Tracy. We watched as it left Tracy, whirling in the sky. It was a sight forever etched in our minds. Tracy survived and has grown. Many new people have moved to Tracy since that day. They have heard many stories of what happened on that day in 1968."

NANCY CRAIG, daughter of Gerald "Brick" and Vivian (Wiggins) Craig lives in Colorado now. This is her account of the tornado: Augustana College's graduation took place on Sunday, June 2, 1968. My B.A. degree represented a major in English (literature) and minors in French and Library Science. Hired by Mr. Vernon Grinde, I was to be the elementary school librarian for the summer session. My salary was funded through a government education program. I was on duty in the library during the hours when teachers, such as my mother, and students were in the building for remedial class work. Mrs. Ruth Grinde, the regular school year librarian, had me do other tasks, to become acquainted with the process of running a real library (for my upcoming position as librarian for two elementary schools in Austin, Mn.) vs. theoretical coursework and internship while I was a Library Science minor at Augustana. I had begun to settle into the school routine when Thursday, June 13 rolled around. Mom and I went to school in the morning, and were back home by lunchtime. As the afternoon wore on, it became increasingly hot and muggy, and by suppertime, it was raining extremely hard. After supper, as usual, I washed the dishes and Mom dried them, with the kitchen radio turned to Marshall's station KMHL for any weather bulletins. I don't remember that the station interrupted its regular programming with much information. It kept raining harder and harder. Suddenly, we heard a car horn honking-honking-honking. A neighbor man, probably Max Lenz or Francis Radke, was driving east on Morgan Street blasting his horn and yelling out the window as he drove. Because of the pounding rain, we never did hear the tornado siren that was screeching downtown, only four blocks away, so that car horn and yelling man were our only "take cover" alert. Based on the neighbor's warning, my parents and I quickly gathered pillows and blankets, my transistor radio and flashlights and went down to our root cellar. By now KMHL radio was reporting that a large funnel had touched down southwest of Tracy and it was headed to make a direct hit on the town. In our basement, we didn't hear the loudest sounds-like-a-freight-train roar of the storm, yet within about ten (?) minutes, we seemed to know that the storm had passed. We and our neighbors popped up out of basements to see the white tornado whirling off to the northeast. Our friend, John Ahrens took one of the definitive photos, used by newspapers across the state, and noted the tornado's exit time as 7:04 P.M. We knew we needed to check on Aunt Ruth and Uncle Bill Craig, a dear family friend who lived across from St, Mary's Church, and other people. We walked near the two school buildings. The high school building seemed OK, but "oh dear" the elementary school was in shambles. The next morning dawned eerily quiet. After breakfast we decided to explore the town. Despite all the damaged homes, the one image that sticks most in my mind is the grade school building, looking as if it had suffered a bomb explosion. We could identify my Mom's 3rd grade classroom on the northwest corner of the middle story. As I recall, when the building was inspected, there were textbooks sitting in order on storage rooms shelves, even if the walls of the room were completely demolished and pieces of chalk sitting on their rails on blackboards; and paperclips and rubber bands in desk drawers. In one classroom the students' desks were still in rows. Shades were still rolled up and hanging-by the now glass-less large windows. Do I recall the clock in my mother's room was stopped at 7:03 – a minute before John Ahrens took his famous photograph? Sometime during that day or the next, school administration members and civic leaders met to determine where and how K-6 classes would be held the following September. Plans were quickly put in place for Sunday school rooms at churches around town, plus St. Mary's offered rooms in their school. What about the library? Hmm, how about using a corner of the high school study hall and "just" move the elementary school buildings over there? But that meant we'd have to remove all the books and shelves from the basement of the horribly damaged grade school building. A call went out to nearby towns to bring men, Boy Scout troops, and hundreds and hundreds of cardboard boxes. A few days later, a work crew was assembled. We began in one corner, at the lowest numbers of the Dewey Decimal System; took books off shelves and put them into boxes. Each box was numbered

(I through XXXX) for when it was time to re-assemble the library over at the high school. As boxes were filled they were passed along a "bucket brigade" through the room, up and out through a window where more people were in another line to move the boxes along to be loaded onto trucks. My Mother was a Nervous Nelly the entire day of this work, knowing there were tons of debris sitting above the library, and the weight of that debris could shift and cause the upper stories to collapse at any moment. Within a few hours we completely emptied the library and everyone got out safely at the end of the day. Evidently, the workmen at the high school (receiving truckloads of books and shelves) hadn't been given explicit instructions: assemble the shelving, then wait for Nancy to arrive the next day to supervise first their placement and secondly the unloading of the boxes of books. Nope. They took it upon themselves (and I'll probably never know who they were!) to DUMP all the books out of all the boxes. When I arrived the next day, there was virtually a pyramid of books filling one corner of the study hall. What? Hardly any two books that belonged next to each other on a bookshelf were found together in the huge pile. Well, at least it was job security for the remainder of the summer; locating books of common Dewey numbers and placing them in the correct order on the shelves. Absolutely every book had to be opened; its pages fanned to check for glass shreds or other debris, then it was dusted before being placed on the shelf. I know that I had helpers but can't remember who they were; adults and / or school children. However, by the time I left for Austin in mid – August, the Tracy grade school library was in place and ready for its opening day of its 1968-69 term.

LINDA GUILD lives in Tracy now. She lived in Slayton in 1968. Her brother, Jim Bakker lived in Tracy and worked at the 7-UP bottling company. They lived where the present water tower is. The tornado blew out all their windows. His wife barely got the basement door shut, but there was glass in her hair. It was several hours before Linda could contact the Red Cross to find out if they were alright. Jim was on his way home from his route. The police weren't going to let him in until they learned that his family was in Tracy. In these 42 years since the tornado, the railroad has diminished. Linda remembers businesses that are no longer here. Some of these were the A and W and J.C. Penney's.

DEB BOULTON was the daughter of Pat and Jerry Stoneberg. Deb says: "I was 12 at the time and my brother Brad who still lives south of Tracy was about a year and a half. I remember after supper that night (June 13) that my dad was worried about hail. He worked for Salmon Chevrolet and left the house to go down to the Chevy garage and put some of the new cars inside. We lived at 236 Harvey St. at that time. He arrived back home and then all of a sudden the civil defense siren was blowing, the sky was sunny and it was hailing! I was always afraid of storms and I suggested we go to the basement. So my folks picked up my brother and I was behind them as I stopped to pick up his favorite blanket. My folks told me to stay with him in this little room where we kept our canned goods, etc. My folks then opened up the doors to our walk up basement and suddenly I heard them say, "Oh, here it comes." I still remember those doors slamming, the lights going off and all of us sitting in that room. I remember that I thought we were going to die as it sounded like a freight train was driving over our heads. It seemed like it lasted forever when it probably was only a minute or two. We stayed in the basement a short time afterwards. Then we came up the stairs. Our house was still there, but as we looked around we noted a one-ton beam in our yard that had blown over a mile from the new high school that was being built. Also, a large rock about a foot in diameter sitting just below our bay window on our open front porch. As we walked outside and looked at the hail on the ground and realized what had happened, I noticed my bicycle was still there and standing! What an amazing thing to have a one-ton beam in your yard and your measly bicycle was still standing where you had left it. I remember not having electricity or water for several days. I remember my dad coming home for brief periods of time and the sticker that was on the inside of his window on the car that gave him clearance to the areas that were hit. He helped find and haul people most of the night. My mother's aunt and uncle drove to Tracy from Sleepy Eye to see if we were OK. They were not allowed into the town. There were no cell phones and all the telephone lines were busy. I remember being in the house and going into a room and turning the light switch on and not remembering that there was no electricity. I had a good friend (Nelda Alexander) who lived across the street and over from the Catholic Church. Her house was lifted up off its foundation and back down again. I remember being amazed at all the destruction, trees downed, the railroad cars lifted off the tracts and blown a block or two. I also remember being amazed at how the Catholic Church and school survived the major destruction. I think I was completely awed at the entire area around 6th street as we used to live on 6th street when we moved to Tracy. The Stantons lived there when I left Tracy in 1974. I don't know who lives there now. There was a lot to clean up and I remember all the people who came from who knows where to see all the destruction. Nine people died. I knew of some of them, but did not personally know them. When I think about all of this, it seems like yesterday and so fresh. Even though it was 42 years ago.

KOREEN ZIEMKE still lives in Tracy. This is her article that was in the paper.

After the tornado came through, only one wall of her family's house was left standing — and it was standing on the lot next door.

"You can see the phone was still on the wall, and the curtains," Ziemke said, looking at a photo taken by her older sister Janet. Only hours before, the Ziemkes had been celebrating their mother Betty's 40th birthday. But a surprise party and a trip to South Dakota turned into a run for survival.

Family photos from that day show Betty and her sisters celebrating with a cake in the dining room of her home in the Greenwood neighborhood of Tracy.

"My sisters and sisters-in-law lived in South Dakota, they came down for the day," Betty Ziemke said.

After the party, they insisted on taking her to Sioux Falls to watch the auto races.

"I didn't want to go," she said. "I just had this feeling I shouldn't leave home, and I shouldn't leave the children."

It was 17-year-old Janet who finally packed Betty's bag and convinced her to go on the trip. She and Koreen, then 13, were left in charge of their younger siblings, Robert, 8, Kathy, 6, Billy, 4, and two-and-a-half-year-old Arlo Jr. As the evening went on, it started to hail, and the kids were catching hailstones in an ice cream bucket.

"At first the only warning we got was a car driving past honking the horn," Koreen Ziemke said. The driver was yelling, "There's a tornado coming!"

The kids huddled in the inside hallway of the house. That was where their father had always told them to go during storms, since they didn't have a basement.

"My older sister Janet said, 'This just doesn't feel right. Let's go over to Domine's,'" Ziemke said.

Janet and Koreen tried to hustle their brothers and sister across the street to the home of Erwin and Dolores Domine, while the tornado came closer.

"As we were running, we saw it take a couple houses," she said. "We were running and it felt like we didn't get anywhere. I still have dreams like that, where I'm running and not moving."

"It was hard. The kids were screaming and fighting, I think some were trying to go back in the house. Janet just said, 'Run,'" Koreen Ziemke said. Even she was dumbstruck for a moment.

Janet alerted the Domine family to the tornado, and they all headed back out and around the Domines' house to the root cellar.

"As we tried to go into the cellar, the door was being blown out of our hands," she said. "It sounded like a train going over."

Coming back up after the twister had passed, Koreen said she could barely recognize her own neighborhood.

"Before, it had been kind of wet and muddy from the rain, but after the tornado, it was just as dry as could be. It was dusty - there was this dust everywhere, and it was kind of weird," she said. "There were live wires jumping everywhere, cars in trees, dogs in trees. It looked like a war zone. I wondered, is this what (my brother) David is going through in Vietnam? That was what I first thought."

"I remember just walking out and seeing everyone standing like, 'What do we do? Where do we go?'" she said. "You feel empty. You feel homeless. We were homeless."

Meanwhile, Betty Ziemke had only made it as far as her sister Lucy's house in South Dakota before stopping to check back home. While at Lucy's, they received a phone call, "saying that there was a bad storm in Tracy and everyone's over to (Kenneth) Anderson's," Betty Ziemke said. "Later they said that was the last call out of Tracy, so that was lucky. We flew back into town."

When Ziemke got back to Tracy, she said, "The National Guard wouldn't let us in at first. I said that I lived there, and he (the Guardsman) said, 'Not anymore.'"

Betty Ziemke found her children and the Domine family unhurt, "But we still had to look for my aunt Millie."

Ziemke's aunt, Mildred Harden, was severely injured and died en route to the hospital. She and her husband Charles had been out on their back porch when the tornado hit.

"They had trees all around the yard, so they couldn't see anything," Betty Ziemke said. "They would always sit and watch the sun set together at a certain time."

"My uncle said (the tornado) came too fast, and he just hung on to her."

The younger children went to stay with relatives that summer, while Janet and her parents remained in Tracy to go through the remains of their house.

"A lot of times all I could think was, 'There goes my everything,'" Betty Ziemke said. "That song was real popular then."

Janet found the camera she used at the birthday party and used it to take pictures of the ruins.

That fall, the Ziemkes ended up moving into the Domine family's old house, the same one where the kids had sought shelter in the cellar. Koreen Ziemke said she remembered going to school in the temporary classrooms set up around town after the tornado. Being gone that summer had messed up her class schedule, she said, but beyond that not much had changed.

"It was exciting, it wasn't a sad thing," she said. "Nobody really talked about (the tornado)."

But life did change for their family. Everyone had a different reaction to the storm. Koreen Ziemke said her younger sister Kathy didn't remember anything from the tornado, while Arlo Jr. would start to cry whenever he heard the vacuum cleaner.

"Every time there's a tornado warning, I think about it all over again," Ziemke said.

The biggest change was to the neighborhood. Many of the families whose homes were destroyed moved away, Betty Ziemke said. For the ones who stayed, there was never the same sense of community as before.

But Ziemke said the experience strengthened her faith, and in a way the tornado united Greenwood to the rest of Tracy. Before, she said, "We were from the other side of the tracks." Things do not change; we change.

MIKE CLARK is my son. This is what he writes.

On June 13, 1968 my family and I were living on a farm place two miles west of Chandler Minnesota. I was only eleven years old at the time, but I still have vivid memories about the Tracy Tornado. My mother's family was from Tracy and we had many relatives who lived there. I remember that we had storms in the area that afternoon and evening and I recall seeing some impressive big billowing thunderheads off to our north that evening. Early the next morning (June 14), my mom and a family friend gathered up my brothers and I and headed to Tracy to find out if any of our relatives were hurt or needed our help. When we arrived at the edge of Tracy, we were stopped by a National Guard soldier. When mom told him that she had family in Tracy, the soldier allowed us to enter town. The tornado had ripped a block and a half wide path through town, entering near the southwest corner of town (in Greentown) and exiting from the north side of town. As we made our way through town, we saw a lot of damage to homes, trees, buildings, autos and other property. I remember seeing a multi-level home with the outside walls ripped away exposing the interior furniture and bathtub. There were twisted trees and rubbish laying everywhere. Stories of my relatives' experiences are included in mom's first book.

OTHER: The following pages include some anonymous contributions, as well as some photos of Tracy today.

FOR YOUR BOOK

June 13, 1968 -- TRACY TORNADO

At 6:55 P.M. Mrs. Melven Koch alerted the Tracy Police that a tornado was approaching the town. The siren was immediately sounded and blew until the power went off at 7:04 P.M. This warning gave many people an opportunity to take cover and undoubtedly saved many lives. Below is a brief- ? - resume of what happened.

The population of Tracy was - 2882. The tornado was about 13 miles long with a main core of 250 feet wide - and approximately another 125 feet of lesser intensity on each side of the core. There were 15 farms damaged - 63 homes completely destroyed - 3 trailer homes carried away - 14 homes partially damaged- 34 homes were later condemmed. In all 162 homes were affected in some way. There were also 250 cars damaged. This represented about 20% of the homes in Tracy.

Of the nine people killed - 6 had no basement - 2 were in cars - 1 was attempting to reach shelter.

Immediately after the tornado had passed the Police Chief and his Civil Defense staff, assisted by the volunteer fire department and other volunteer citizens - took charge. They were soon joined by the Sheriff of the county and the National Guard.

A communication center was set up in the Municipal Building. By midnight a short wave communication center had been set up in the Armory. Housing information was set up in the municipal building. A list of those who could provide tempory shelter was compiled within the first 24 hours .

During the five days following the disaster 2,039 volunteers were recorded as working in the town and outlying areas. Contractors donated trucks, tractors, and bulldozers. A local bulk trucker - donated and supplied trucks with gas. In the rural areas - 200 school children working with 4H group leaders - and county agents - criss-crossed all affected fields loading trucks with debris. Other agencies assisting - Seventh Day Advents - Salvation Army - Red Cross - local clubs and organizations, and many citizen volunteers.

Phone service and electricity were restored the following day. Although the the water tower was not destroyed - water was not available for the following 24 hours. Water was hauled in from neighboring towns.

It should be pointed out here that many more lives could have been lost as the grade school was badly damaged.

Following is the Hospital Story:

Tracy Municipal Hospital is a one story building opened in 1962, with a bed capacity of 42. At the time of the tornado there were 3 physicians on the staff. One retired physician living in town. The census that night was 35 and there were five nurses on duty on the 3-11 shift. 23 patients were admitted during the night making a total of 58 up to midnight. After midnight there was one young girl admitted with hystera and one miscarriage. There were no babies in the nursery at the time and none admitted during the next days. All elective surgery was cancelled for one week. Outpatients seen, treated, and released the first night were 77 at the hospital. Later the following day and aide station was set up down town.

Although phone numbers of employees were readily available, there was no phone service. However by the time the first patient had arrived employees returning to duty were on hand to care for casulaties. No hospital employee was notified, all returned, and those on vacation were back by the next day.

Nurses were registered from as far away as Huron, So. Dak. and Duluth, Minn. An exact list of those assisting the first night is not available, however the next few days those assisting were as follows:

6-14-68   12 R.N.   8 L.P.N.

6-15-68   7 R.N.   8 L.P.N.

6-16-68   16 R.N.   6 L.P.N.

Volunteers as much as possible were either assigned to work with a local nurse or were assigned to special the more seriously injured tornado victims.

By Monday the 17th, although volunteers continued to arrive the number had lessened and we felt that we were able to "stand on our own feet".

The types of injuries encountered were:

1. Fractured vertebraes. (3 of these were later fitted with Taylor Brace)

2. Fractured limbs.

3. Chest injuries - one had a tracheostomy later.

4. Lacerations and abrasions.

5. Puncture wounds - nails/- nails/- nails/

One week after the tornado 171 tornado "related" patients had been seen in the outpatient department. Of these, 40 were nail punctures, 33 were small laceration and or abrasions. Other types of injuries or illness registered were: dog bites; horse bites; constipation; and asthma like symotoms which later developed into a productive cough, the secretions being black and tarry.

The hospital disaster plan was placed into effect immediately. Extra beds were placed in 124,123, 110, solarium, and later cots were placed on one side of the corridor in the East wing. Only one family asked/of a private room "for Auntie". Surgery personnel set up extra suture sets- consisting of scissors, needle holder, clamp, tissue forceps. These were cold sterilized after use. More extensive suturing was done with the minor sets.

The standby generator provided lights in the emergency room, operating room, and patient area. The hospital dinning room which has a large glass window was used as a "triage" area. There was plenty of light from the window. A generator was brought in before morning and the power was restored to the hospital.

Patients begin arriving immediately - coming in trucks, cars, ambulances, on doors. The first patient to arrive was an elderly diabetic.. This lady had a slight insulin reaction during the nite which was corrected with food as she had not had her evening meal.

It was decided by Administration that doors would not be locked and that people would be permitted to enter. A guard was posted at the entrances to direct traffic and to keep the ambulance entrance clear.

Auxiliary members assisted in registering patients, especially those less seriously injured who were waiting in the front lobby. Auxilians also assisted in the kitchen, and one member remained at the nurses station answering the phone and issuing information.

Laundry, was sent out for a few days, and extra linen was sent in from another hospital so that clean linen was never a problem.

Passes were issued to workers, and those from other towns took passes back for other volunteers arriving for a later shift.

Three members of the "hospital family" lost their homes. All returned to workm some as early as the night of the tornado. It was of interest to note that employees had time to have coffee for these members and to share with thema a gift of money, food, and household goods.

Below are some of the "problems" and how they were handled:

1. Lights - flashlights were wsed - an extra supply were brought by Civil Defense. Water - at a minimum - Zephirin wash and dri wipes were used.

   Comment: At the first indication of a - tornado watch - all bath tubs are now filled with water.

2. Out patient slips were found to be quite fragile - they have been replaced with a sturdy three part cardboard disaster tag. Box which is kept in the emergency room also contains safety pins, and pen and pencils. It was found that many people who came just as they were did not have pens.

   Comment: At a subsequent evaluation session it was decided to place the disaster plan into effect for any accident involving 4 or more people. We would use the disaster tags, and bring stretchers to ambulance entrance so that this would become "habit" and relieve key people for other duties.

3. An immediate check of Dextran, Penicillin, and Tetanus was made. One of the first contingent of Physicians arriving from a nearby town brought Tetanus and Penicillin with them.

4. Paper tape was found to work faster than regular wrist bands. Large yellow x-ray paper was used to mark beds with special instructions;

i.e. Keep bed flat! This on those with fractured vertebraes. This
was helpful for those volunteering from other hospitals.

5. Washing and bathing of routine patients was kept to a minimum at first,
the availabe water and time was spent in cleaning the black oily sub-
stance off skin and hair. It was found after repeated washings ears
were always dirty.

6. Ten days after the tornado, one lady developed Tetanus. She had
recieved routine Tetanus Toxoid as had all the injured; however she
had never been immunized previously. It was decided to periodically
remind all employees and especially after accidents to review the signs
and symptoms of Tetanus.

7. A list of patients was kept on file at the information desk and at the
nurses station. This consisted of :

   Those treated and released.

   Those admitted.

   Those DOA and mortuary where they were taken.

   Those missing. (one ex-member of the hospital family was reported
   missing for a time.)

   Later this list also included those dismissed and address where
   they could be found.

8. A separate file was kept of torando victums treated in outpatient.
The out patient which normally is staffed by O.R. and after 3PM by floor
nurses, was staffed until 11PM for 1 week. It was found that volunteers
and workers engaged in cleaning worked late and many times came in
between 10 and 11PM. Standing orders were to cleanse, soak in phis-
ohex, dress, and give Tetanus Toxoid. Any unusual injuries were
referred to physician. (The nurses was one who had expierence in surgery)

9. Extra help was provided in the kitchen and also three ladies volunteered
to come at meal tome and serve trays and feed patients. This was
very helpful.

10. After the volunteer physicians had left, patients were assigned to local
    Doctors by:

    1. Those they had treated.

    2. Patient preference

    3. Whose patients they had been previously.

    Lists were ready by 7AM and charts were ready by 7AM.

11. Extra utensils were borrowed from local nursing homes, as well as beds,
    and screens.

12. Kenny Rehab. sent two people down to evaluate and assist.

13. Western Mental Health came down on several occasions to visitand assist.

14. An unforgetful experience.

<u>July 17, 1968</u>   As an aftermath of the tornado the Red Cross held a Disaster
conference at Christian Manor - this was attended by LPN and RN staff members.
As this as not open to nurse aides - it was felt that this information
would be presented to them also. This was done in an afternoon meeting at the
hospital.

THE BULLETIN of the

ST. LOUIS PARK MEDICAL CENTER

EDITOR — DONALD A. DUNCAN, M.D.

ASSOCIATE EDITORS

JAMES C. DAHL, M.D.   FRED E. MECKLENBURG, M.D.

HUGH A. EDMONDSON, JR., M.D.   RICHARD C. WOELLNER, M.D.

VOLUME XII   SUMMER QUARTER 1968   NUMBER 3

CONTENTS

A NIGHT OF TERROR IN TRACY
     By Earl G. Yonehiro, M.D., Ph.D., F.A.C.S. *
     S. R. Maxeiner, Jr., M.D., F.A.C.S. **
Department of Surgery 39

SYMPTOM CHECK LIST: AN AID TO REPORTING
TEACHER OBSERVATIONS IN MINIMAL BRAIN
DYSFUNCTION
     By Arnold S. Anderson, M.D.
Department of Pediatrics 47

*Chairman, Subcommittee on Disaster Medicine, Minnesota Committee on
     Trauma, American College of Surgeons

**Chairman, Minnesota Committee on Trauma, American College of Surgeons.
     Private Practice, General Surgery, Minneapolis, Minnesota

4959 Excelsior Boulevard, Minneapolis, Minn. 55416

A NIGHT OF TERROR IN TRACY

Earl G. Yonehiro, M. D., Ph. D., F.A.C.S., *
and
S. R. Maxeiner, Jr., M. D., F.A.C.S. **

DEPARTMENT OF SURGERY

The evening of June 17, 1968 was warm and muggy with ominous dark clouds filling the skies. The wind strengthened and hail as large as lemons began falling. The hail storm was quickly replaced by a soft rain which grew in intensity and then abruptly stopped, leaving an eerie silence. What happened in the next 25 minutes will never be forgotten by the residents of a small farming area in southwestern Minnesota.

A farm lady, Mrs. Melvin Koch, living one mile east of Garvin, Minnesota first sighted the frightening tornado funnel heading slowly, in a northeasterly direction, toward the town of Tracy. She quickly contacted and alerted the Tracy radio dispatcher, Julius De Blieck, who immediately set off the alert siren at 6:55 p.m. The siren screeched its warning to the citizenry of Tracy until 7:04 p.m. when all power failed. The fact that the alert signal was given enabled most of the people in Tracy to take cover in the basement of their homes. This undoubtedly saved many lives. The sound of the tornado was described as a weird, frightening "roar of a freight train without the clickety-click." For 25 minutes the tornado cut a swath of destruction in the vicinity of Tracy ten miles long and 2-1/2 blocks wide passing through the town from a southwesterly direction and disappearing into the northeast fields. It left in its destructive wake 9 dead and 72 injured of whom 22 required hospitalization.

The subsequent 72 hours displayed magnificently the spirit and courage of the townspeople and the community at large, which responded to the urgent call of mercy.

This report is an analysis of some of the pertinent aspects of the disaster, the medical care rendered and the process of rebuilding.

The town of Tracy, Minnesota is located approximately 150 miles southwest of the Twin Cities and has a population of 2,882. The tornado completely demolished 63 homes and so damaged 14 more that they subsequently were torn down. An additional 34 homes were condemned. In lesser degree 81 other homes were damaged. These homes represented 20% of the town's residences.

Immediately after the disaster Police Chief, Merle Kathman, took charge of the disaster area with help from his department, the volunteer fire department and citizen volunteers. Almost immediately the County Sheriff's organization and National Guard units moved in to augment civil units.

A two-way radio was available and help was requested from the nearby towns of Slayton and Marshall including two-way radios and auxiliary power generators, which were quickly brought in. A communications center was set up in the Municipal Building. By midnight a ham radio operator and some local

*Chairman, Subcommittee on Disaster Medicine, Minnesota Committee on Trauma, American College of Surgeons.
**Chairman, Minnesota Committee on Trauma, American College of Surgeons. Private Practice, General Surgery, Minneapolis, Minnesota.

explorer scouts had set up a short wave radio communications center in the Armory chiefly to contact relatives of town residents. The telephone lines were down. Volunteer groups from Waseca brought two-way radio equipment to direct work crews and others throughout the disaster area.

A housing information . . . . ed in the Municipal Building for those whose . . . . were destro . . . . were taken in by local people. A list of persons who could provide temporary shelter was made during the first 24 hours.

Because of the tremendous army of volunteers who came into town to help, the work of reconstruction began almost immediately. Radio stations in Marshall, Pipestone and Worthington, and WCCO in Minneapolis, by broadcasting the needs for specific equipment and machinery necessary to clear the debris, were extremely helpful. For example, within an hour after a call for chain saws went over the air the city was deluged with them. Requests for trucks, clothing, refrigerators and household appliances made over the air resulted in adequate supplies being donated within hours. During the five days following the disaster 2,039 volunteers were recorded as working in the town and outlying areas.

The Municipal Government, headed by Dr. Jack Von Bockern, an Optometrist and President of the City Council, decided that the cost of clearing and removing the debris from the disaster area should be done with public funds. However, because of the large number of volunteers and the private contribution of equipment and supplies the actual expenditure for the clean-up was amazingly small. Contractors donated trucks, tractors and bulldozers. Construction workers volunteered their time to the city for the clean-up. A local bulk petroleum dealer with a two-way radio replenished gasoline for the vehicles working on the clean-up and reconstruction. In the rural areas over a period of 5 days 200 school children working with 4-H groups and County Agents criss-crossed all fields affected by the tornado loading trucks with debris. Groups of these children would meet in the morning at their assigned fields. The Red Cross and Salvation Army provided snacks at work and local buses brought the children to town for lunch. Their being outside the town while working helped relieve the congestion within the town.

Phone service and electricity were restored in the city by the following day. Although the city water tower was not destroyed, its water was not available for a period of 24 to 48 hours. Therefore it was necessary to haul in water from surrounding areas for sanitary and personal uses. When city water did become available there was some apprehension among the town people about its possible contamination.

One problem in the clean-up aspect of the disaster was the city dump, for within a few days the rubbish and debris that was collected completely filled it.

The Police Chief in view of his experience during the crisis made the following observations:

1. Numerous two-way radios were essential.
2. There should be auxiliary generator units available in the Municipal buildings as well as in the hospital.
3. Control of persons admitted to the disaster area by early issuance of passes is essential.
4. A central communication organization and a depot to supply necessary household living needs are a necessity during the crisis period.

5. Outside aid from volunteer groups to rapidly clean up the area is necessary and was the greatest single factor in re-establishing order from the chaos.

Mr. . . . . during the disaster period indicated that the greatest task ahead was to provide new housing for the elderly. A large number of the homes destroyed were those of . . . . The Department of Housing and Urban Development has facilitated the processing of applications for 60 units for housing for the elderly. The projected start on this construction is January, 1969.

Mr. Con Rettner also observed that during the clean-up period there was a need for a portable tire repair unit. The streets being littered with nails and debris caused numerous flat tires on the trucks and other vehicles with a resultant loss of a large amount of time and effort. He felt that in another similar situation such a unit would help greatly in meeting this mechanical problem.

Dr. Jack Von Bockern, President of the City Council, felt that the single most fortunate aspect of the disaster was that the Municipal Hospital had been spared, noting that the nearest hospital otherwise was 25 miles away (either Slayton or Marshall). The difficulties inherent in providing medical care in Tracy without the hospital, and in attempting to transport the injured to the nearest hospitals the night of the tornado would have been most serious.

The magnitude of the disaster was illustrated by newspaper photographs showing boxcars lying in intersections of streets four blocks from railroad tracks, many devastated homes, huge uprooted trees and a mild array of downed telephone and electrical lines. Insured damages of $2,000,000 to private homes and $750,000 to public buildings have been assessed. Uninsured property losses are estimated at an additional $1,250,000.

At the present time, some three weeks after the disaster, Tracy, which had been uprooted and partially destroyed, has made a remarkable recovery thanks to a bit of luck, the tremendous courage of its towns-people and to the great numbers of volunteers who came from afar to give help.

EMERGENCY MEDICAL CARE AND DISASTER MEDICINE

The Tracy Municipal Hospital, built in 1962, is a pleasant, modern, air conditioned structure with 42 beds. Three active physicians and 35 part and full-time nurses staff it. The medical staff consists of Drs. Norman J. Lee, Roger Schroeppel and Patrick Bosley. Dr. Charles W. Graham, a radiologist from Spirit Lake, Iowa comes in once a week.

In the aftermath of the tornado 111 patients were registered and either hospitalized or released after treatment. All 35 nurses answered the call for help and many volunteer nurses came, some from as far away as Duluth. Four physicians from Marshall, four from Slayton and two doctors from Pipestone came to help out within the first hours. Two other physicians vacationing in the area also participated in the emergency. Help if needed was volunteered by physicians as far away as Dallas, Texas.

For Dr. Norman J. Lee it was a night he will not forget. An amateur photographer, he took pictures of the approaching tornado as well as movies of the storm. These were subsequently used by Walter Cronkite on his CBS program. Dr. Lee recalls the terrifying high pitched constant whine of the siren intermingled with the roar of the oncoming tornado. When the electrical power went

Photograph of the approaching tornado funnel taken by
Dr. Norman J. Lee of Tracy, Minnesota

off and the siren stopped, he felt an odd personal sense of abandonment by civilization. As soon as the storm passed, his home not having been damaged, Dr. Lee went directly to the hospital.

Most of the injured who did not survive the tornado were killed outright. . . . . were in extremis when brought to the hospital and died sh. . . . . . . after. One had . . . . ghost and f. an evisceration. The majority of the patients had numerous wounds from flying glass. Many had abrasions and contusions from falling objects and there were some burns. Approximately 20 per cent of the patients had sustained orthopedic injuries. Representative of these were three compound fractures of the spine, a fractured jaw, fractured ribs, three fractured tibias and a trimalleolar fracture. The skin of most of the patients was black from dirt and many had been tattooed with dirt and particulate matter. Interestingly one patient subsequently developed tetanus. His macerated leg had been treated by the open method, in addition to which he had received care for numerous minor lacerations. At the initial treatment he had been given tetanus toxoid, Hypertet® and antibiotics. This patient is still hospitalized and a favorable prognosis has been given.

All patients were sent to the Municipal Hospital. They came in ambulances, on stretchers and on makeshift stretchers of doors and boards. The dead were placed in the hospital laundry room which was used as a temporary morgue. Tags with pertinent information were used on all patients, and the routine admission sheet was used for additional immediate data. Since the physicians knew many of the patients personally much of the medical data was readily recalled and posted later in the charts. Essentially the diagnosis, suturing of lacerations, general condition and medications were entered on the tag and signed by the physician. Tetanus toxoid shots were given almost routinely to patients who entered the emergency room. The following day the county health nurse gave tetanus boosters at the Municipal Building to a large number of the townspeople.

Cots, beds and supplies were sent to the hospital from the Christian Manor Nursing Home and from Tracy, Incorporated, both 60 bed nursing homes. These were placed in the corridors and patient rooms. The solarium, lobby and dining rooms were also used for patients whose care could be delayed. Some of these had their lacerations sutured the following day.

Only one patient had major surgery done the first evening. This person had multiple injuries including a skull fracture, extensive ankle injuries and numerous severe lacerations of her body.

Although the hospital proper had auxiliary generators for electricity the emergency room did not; consequently two generators were brought from adjacent towns. Because many patients brought in were coated with dirt the nursing and volunteer personnel contributed significantly by washing and cleaning up the wounds. All patients in extremis were isolated and had nurses assigned to them. Major fractures, such as trimalleolar and tibial fractures, requiring surgery were pinned by a surgeon the following day. Even a veterinarian assisted in suturing lacerations. Fortunately none of the physicians in town was injured and none of the medical facilities of Tracy was affected by the tornado.

Although a formal disaster plan was available for the hospital and had been discussed periodically by the nursing and administrative staff there had not been any formal drills. It was not utilized, as such, by the medical staff. But, two years earlier a bus-truck accident had occurred six miles west of Tracy. At that time 41 teenagers were injured and two died. The medical staff had learned much from that experience about handling mass casualties, and that knowledge was an important factor in the successful management of the tornado disaster. Also in paramount importance was that a large inventory of suture material, dressings, parenteral fluids and blood substitutes was available in the hospital.

Two local blood bank technicians were aided by others from outlying communities. Laboratory work was thus carried out expeditiously. The most common lab work was CBC's and urinalyses. Because of the water shortage, glassware could not be cleaned and distilled water was brought in since community water was not available for 48 hours. The Red Cross Blood Bank in St. Paul and the blood bank of the hospital in Marshall supplied needed units of blood.

Dr. Charles W. Graham, Radiologist, who flew in the same evening of the tornado from Spirit Lake, Iowa contributed significantly to the medical care. He worked tirelessly with others until the following day.

Dr. Patrick Bosley, a physician from Balaton, Minnesota, stated that the greatest deficiency noted during the emergency was the lack of adequate electric power and generators to satisfactorily run the entire hospital including the emergency room and operating room. Not until generators were brought in from Granite Falls was this problem alleviated. The second deficiency he noted was the lack of adequate reserve amounts of water for hospital care necessitating water to be hauled in by trucks. Other than for these two points he had nothing but praiseworthy comments for the entire medical and paramedical staff, from the kitchen help through the nursing personnel, the technicians and the physicians for the splendid cooperation and great amount of energy and talent that they contributed.

Dr. Lee who acted as the physician in charge emphasized:

1. The importance of stock piling supplies to meet any emergency.
2. The good fortune in being swamped with volunteers of all talent and variety.
3. There is no substitute for actual experience in terms of meeting a disaster and that the prior bus-truck accident had indeed provided this.
4. The need for a specific physician to take charge to minimize confusion.

An interesting observation of Dr. Lee is that approximately one week following the tornado he began to see patients for a severe dry bronchitic cough and chest discomfort. Subsequently the cough became productive and the secretions were tarry black. He estimated that 40-50 patients were seen by him for this type of respiratory distress. Approximately six developed bronchopneumonia. It is presumed that particulate matter inhaled during the storm caused this unusual condition.

NURSING CARE

Miss Nellie Wright, Director of Nursing, went directly to the hospital as soon as the tornado had passed. By the time casualties started coming numerous volunteer nurses had arrived on the scene. All worked for long hours throughout the period of need. Miss Wright has made recommendations to the hospital administration as follows:

1. There is a need for standby power.
2. Guards must be posted early at   times so   the area clea. o. .on-injured persons who tend to congregate there.
3. Persons not concerned with the care of patients must be kept out of the hospital for they impede efficient emergency care.
4. Extra suture trays and instruments for immediate wound closure should be available in the hospital inventory.
5. A single large tag should be used for each patient for the data required during the early admission and emergency care period. There was too much expenditure of effort filling out the usual admission and care sheets.
6. An accurate census and count of available beds on each hospital floor should be available at all times during the admission period of casualties.
7. There should be a larger stock piling of linen.
8. Paper wrist bands should be used rather than plastic bands.
9. Instructions concerning care of back injuries should be more widely disseminated.
10. Water must be consciously conserved if the supply is limited.

In summary certain factors of utmost importance are noted as contributing to the fine disaster medicine practiced at Tracy.

1. The hospital, the physicians, nurses and all paramedical help escaped injury by the tornado.
2. The siren gave sufficient warning to allow most of the townspeople to seek shelter. No person who sought shelter in a basement was killed although injuries were incurred.
3. Adequate communication with two-way radio was available.
4. Massive volunteer help was at the scene early.
5. Sightseers and other non-productive persons were kept away from the area during the days after the tornado struck.
6. A disaster had previously been experienced by the community and this proved extremely helpful in mobilizing for the emergency.
7. Adequate medical supplies were available.

In the final analysis it was the volunteers, the professionals and nonprofessionals -- all the people with a helping hand and willing heart who provided the compassion and talents necessary for adequate emergency and disaster care.

The following is a list of physicians who gave unselfishly of their time and talents during and following the Tracy tornado.

Staff Doctors: Dr. N. J. Lee, Tracy, Minnesota
                    Dr. P. Bosley, Balaton, Minnesota
                    Dr. R. O. Schroeppel, Tracy, Minnesota
                    Dr. W. G. Workman (retired), Tracy, Minnesota
                    Dr. C. W. Graham, Radiologist, Spirit Lake, Iowa

Volunteer Doctors: Dr. J. E. Eckdale, Marshall, Minnesota
                       Dr. K. A. Peterson, Marshall, Minnesota
                       Dr. R. W. Taintor, Marshall, Minnesota
                       Dr. P. C. Hedenstrom, Marshall, Minnesota

Dr. J. E. Bader, Slayton, Minnesota
Dr. R. F. Pierson, Slayton, Minnesota
Dr. H. Patterson, Slayton, Minnesota
Dr. D. Nywall, Slayton, Minnesota
Dr. R. Kotval, Pipestone, Minnesota
Dr. R. W. Keyes, Pipestone, Minnesota

Also assisting during the night of the tornado were:
Dr. J. B. Sawyer, Dentist, Walnut Grove, Minnesota
Dr. E. K. Bicek, Veterinarian, Tracy, Minnesota

TRACY
AMBULANCE

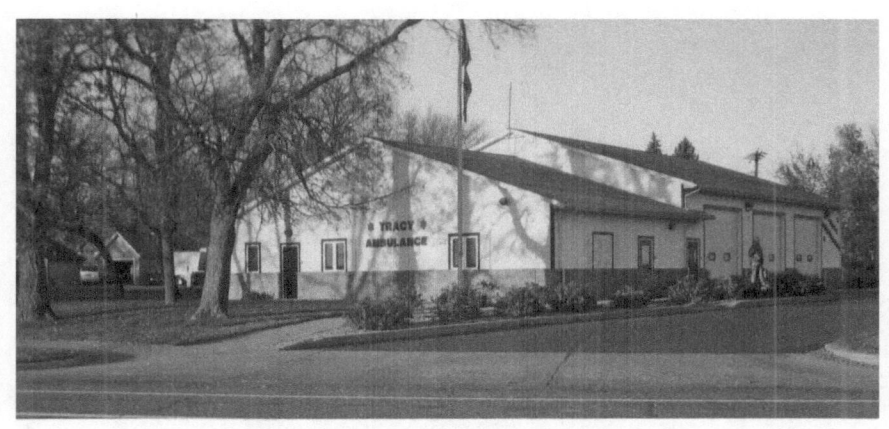

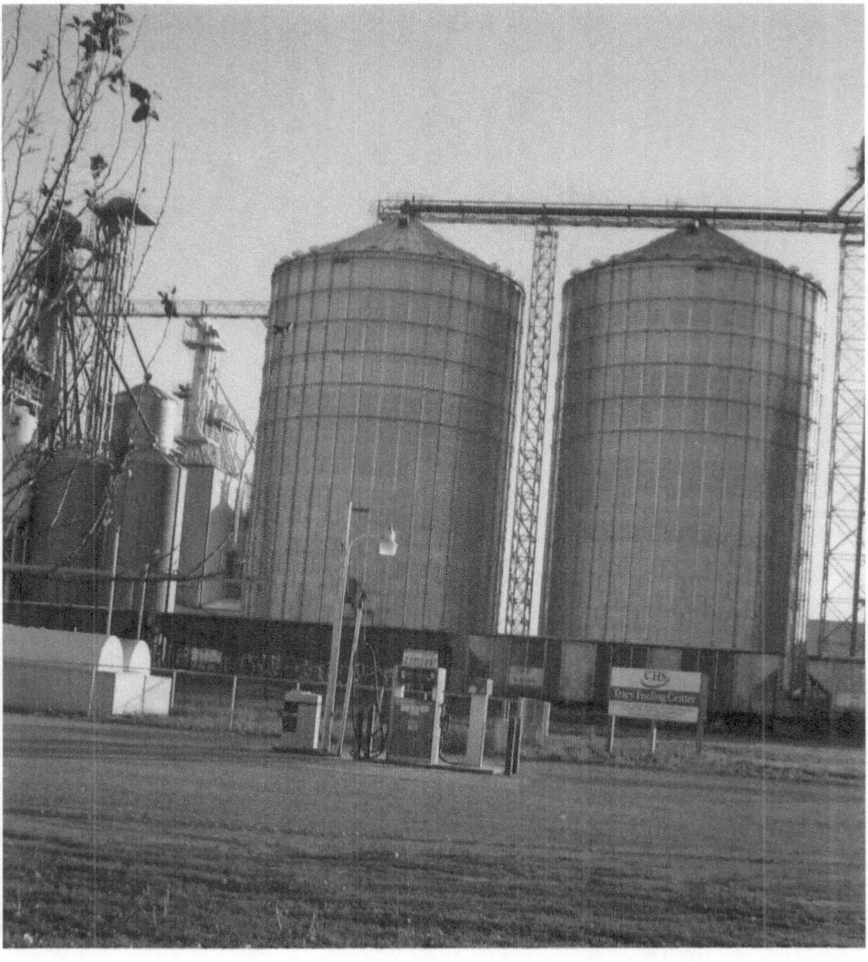
CHS
Tracy Fueling Center

EPILOGUE

43 years have come and gone since the terrible tornado came to Tracy, Minnesota, taking with it nine lives and many homes, schools, trees, automobiles, train cars, property of all sorts, Tracy is still here and many people who survived it still live here. As the years passed by many have only vague memories of that time while it was so life-changing for others that their memories are engraved in their hearts forever. The trains still whistle when they pass through the city, farmers still bring their harvest to the city's elevator. There is one large grocery store, a drug store, a gas station. There are two schools and children who were babies then are now men and women, some with children of their own. Some are even grandparents now. Tracy still celebrates Labor Day, it's annual Box Car Days with a long, colorful parade; with a carnival of rides and food stands. New homes have been built while others have been torn down. The hospital and clinic remain, more modern now. Specialists come from large cities to see patients to keep them from having to travel for many medical needs. The nursing home across from the hospital remains, while a new fitness center is nearby. A large assisted living facility near the hospital is named O'Brien Court. A new very up to date swimming pool attracts many. Down town there are some new businesses and restaurants and churches. As for those who were here on that date in 1968 some still watch the sky when a storm cloud is nearby or wonder when tornado watches forecast whether it would happen here again. Some may shudder at the sound of a siren's blare. Most have made sure that they have a place to go for shelter "just in case." For most of the residents that were living here or nearby that tragic day, however life has gone on and memories begin to fade.